MUSICAL ITALY REVISITED

Monuments and Memorabilia: A Supplement to Guidebooks

MUSICAL ITALY REVISITED

"voci
cantaron sì che nol diria sermone."
(*Purg.* xii. 110–11)

by Siegmund Levarie

THE MACMILLAN COMPANY, NEW YORK
COLLIER-MACMILLAN LIMITED, LONDON

FIRST PRINTING

The Macmillan Company, New York
Collier-Macmillan Canada Ltd., Toronto, Ontario
Library of Congress catalog card number: 63–16111

PRINTED IN THE UNITED STATES OF AMERICA

Acknowledgment is due the following publishers for permission to use copyrighted materials:

American Musicological Society: material from an article by Frank A. D'Accone, "The Singers of San Giovanni in Florence during the 15th Century," published in the *Journal of the American Musicological Society,* XIV/3 (fall, 1961); here used in the chapter on Florence.

The Clarendon Press, Oxford: description of the Teatro San Giovanni Grisostomo in Venice, taken from Simon T. Worsthorne's *Venetian Opera in the Seventeenth Century.*

Dover Publications, Inc., New York: material from Alois M. Nagler's *Source Book in Theatrical History;* here incorporated in the chapters on Venice and Vicenza.

L. B. Fischer and S. Fischer Verlag, Frankfurt-am-Main: excerpts from *Verdi: The Man in His Letters,* edited by Franz Werfel and Paul Stefan, and translated by Edward Downes.

Alfred A. Knopf, Inc., New York: quotations from the *Memoirs of Hector Berlioz,* edited by Ernest Newman.

Macmillan & Co. Ltd., London: excerpts from *The Letters of Mozart and His Family,* edited and translated by Emily Anderson.

W. W. Norton & Company, Inc., New York: documents concerning the *camerata* in Florence, taken from *Source Readings in Music History,* compiled and edited by Oliver Strunk.

Pantheon Books, New York: quotations from *Felix Mendelssohn: Letters,* edited by G. Selden-Goth.

To Janet

a good companion in music and in Italy

Table of Contents

List of Illustrations

(following page 84)

INTRODUCTION

THE AMERICAN TRAVELER in Italy is exposed to a great deal of culture. Whether he wants to or not, he gathers information on European history, Roman architecture, and Renaissance art. The imaginative and curious visitor can easily map out his own special course, tracing, if he wishes, the Byzantine influence from Venice and Ravenna down to Sicily; or the characteristic Jesuit style in church architecture; or the paintings of Pinturicchio; or the spirit of poets in the landscape (as Gilbert Highet has recently done). But although Italy's contribution to music is second to none, the tourist will only rarely be made aware of the musical *genius loci*. Opera was born in Florence. Will the faithful subscriber to the Metropolitan Opera, in his guidebook or on his strolls through town or in his general concern, find the Bardi and Corsi palaces where opera was first conceived and produced in the 1590's? The simultaneous use of two organs and two choirs across the space of St. Mark's Cathedral in Venice was as big an artistic feat as the contemporary organization of space and color by Tintoretto or Veronese. Yet a friendly priest in St. Mark's looked at me with surprise when I asked him whether both organs were played on Sunday mornings. Simultaneously? he shuddered.

One reason for the disproportionate neglect of music in favor of the other arts might lie in the very nature of music. Paintings, sculptures, and buildings come to life as soon as anyone looks at them. Music, on the other hand, remains mute until the traveler uses his inner ear and imagination to wake the Sleeping Beauty. This argument would be more convincing, alas, if poetry shared the fate of music. But there are Virgil monuments and postcards all over Mantua, whereas no homage or even attention is paid to Monteverdi; and a splendid Roman villa in Sirmione is falsely and proudly attributed to Catullus, whose poems are more remote from our common experiences than Baroque sonatas.

The fact remains, for whatever reasons, that music has not penetrated man's general awareness of his cultural history as much as have painting, sculpture, architecture, and poetry. With all the recent popularization of music brought about by radio and phonograph, Josquin Des Prez remains remote and strange to the average person who lines up in a queue to admire the "Mona Lisa" by Leonardo da Vinci, Josquin's contemporary.

A musical guide will carry the burden of this disadvantage. The difficulty is increased by the intangibility and invisibility of the musical experience. To the traveler in Italy, the accumulated musical wealth of the country becomes corporeal in three kinds of buildings. Until about 1600, the musical life of a town was concentrated in the local church (as in Venice) or in the local palace (as in Ferrara). In the seventeenth century, the public theater joined, and later often superseded in importance, the two other musical centers as a full-fledged third partner.

Thus necessarily favoring churches, palaces, and theaters, this book intends to remind the traveler in Italy of the musical heritage of the country and to add a missing musical layer to the other instructive and pleasurable accomplishments of the trip. The book is a musical guide, but of a special kind. Its limits are set by the musical monuments that may be visited as much as by the predilections of the author. It proceeds neither chronologically, like a history book; nor systematically, like a catalogue or a Baedeker; nor with the intent of complete coverage, like a textbook. It is rather directed at the intelligent traveler who is as much interested in music as he is in art. He need not carry it around on his tiring walks through each city, although it might refresh his memory during a rest period at a coffeehouse table. He might profitably read it in bed before turning off the lights the first night in a new town. His aroused curiosity might evoke a rich world otherwise muffled. If the traveler remembers the presence of the musical spirit of the town next day on his wanderings and pauses at this or that place with a fresh idea generated by these pages, the experience will carry its own reward.

A word about the manner in which the location of buildings is identified in the course of the text. Consistent use of street addresses would be correct but impractical. In some cities, like Venice, they barely exist. In others, they are less familiar than references to indicative churches and palaces. Some places, like Lucca, abound in markers; others, like Bologna, maintain reticence. Inconsistencies of spelling and naming often occur within the same block. With all these difficulties in mind, I have chosen to define the location of a building or of an object in terms that are most likely to direct the reader quickly and easily to it. The underlying assumption is that the intelligent traveler does not mind consulting a map or a traffic officer whenever he is at a loss in regard to the obvious landmarks of a community.

An author likes to note his gratitude in print, not merely to express it to the friends who already know of it, but to honor himself by a lasting association. Hugo Kauder, Ernst Levy, and Kamilla Spear read the manuscript and shared with me their reactions. Valborg Anderson, Joseph F. De Simone, and Dante Negro—all colleagues at Brooklyn College—generously and patiently helped me across obstacles in the various fields in which they are experts. Robert W. Wadsworth, of the University of Chicago, stood by for special emergencies. Josef Mertin, of the State Academy for Music in Vienna, led me to the organs in northern Italy; he also produced the illustrations Nos. 1 and 2. Whenever these friends participated, they changed my labor into pleasure.

Strangers, too, were generous. I am singularly indebted to various persons and agencies in Italy for contributing illustrations to this text. The following listing of official credits should be interpreted as an expression of my thankfulness. 3: Studi di Fotografia Allegri, Brescia. 4: Ente Provinciale per il Turismo, Cremona. 5, 6, 7, 9, 11, and 14: Fratelli Alinari, Florence. 8: Ditta Scartabelli, Viareggio. 10: Mario Moretti, Orvieto. 12: Ente Provinciale per il Turismo, Parma. 13: Carlo Cicalese, Ravello. 15: Maria Plazzer, Rovereto. 16: Fondazione Scientifica Querini-Stampalia, Venice.

The information contained in this book is as correct and relevant as an author could make it who is both a music professor and an ardent traveler. The meticulous reader discovering discrepancies between this book and respectable reference works may rest assured that the author is likely to be aware of them. His personal visits and inquiries are of a more recent date, and his information in this instance is likely to be more reliable than library wisdom. But cities change quickly and objects get moved around; relevant comments and corrections by users of this book will be welcomed.

Siegmund Levarie

AREZZO

THE CENTRAL SQUARE of this town, the Piazza Guido Monaco, is named after a musician whose monument stands in the middle. Guido d'Arezzo—Guido the Monk, as his townspeople call him—was a teacher around the year 1000. His influence is still felt today. Trained as a Benedictine monk (the hardest-working order of all) in Pomposa near Ferrara, he had to leave his confreres in mature years because of intrigues against his revolutionary and superior teaching methods. Around that time (1025), Bishop Theobald of Arezzo showed great interest in both music and education. This *episcopus benevolus* hired Guido to teach the choirboys in the cathedral and encouraged him to write down his ideas on music pedagogy. To Bishop Theobald, Guido dedicated the *Micrologus,* a textbook of musical methods, which is still being reprinted (Rome 1955 most recently). No other music treatise was copied so frequently during the Middle Ages. As a result, early manuscripts of the *Micrologus* exist in many libraries. The American need travel no farther than Rochester, New York, to admire a twelfth-century copy in the Sibley Musical Library of the Eastman School of Music; and the Library of Congress in Washington owns a fifteenth-century Codex (identified as ML. 171. J6).

Guido's fame brought him an invitation to Rome, where he explained his methods to the court of Pope John XIX. Eventually he must have encountered difficulties in Arezzo, too, for he moved to the monastery at Avellana in Umbria and ultimately back to Pomposa, where he died around 1050.

The teaching of music to schoolchildren is a problem of which the external details have changed over the centuries (for so have musical styles), but of which the basic principles have remained the same (for so have little boys). Guido applied his good sense for practical devices when he recast his *Micrologus* into easily remembered verse, *Regulae Rhythmicae,* to be memorized by his flock. He displayed supreme musical acumen by concentrating his efforts on those skills which even today should provide the foundation for all musical education: ear-training, sightsinging, and notation. Thus he thought up various exercises and musical games to challenge the attention, while sharpening the ears, of his students. Among his devices is the use of one's left hand (the "Guidonian Hand") in such a manner that any sequence of tones can be read off the joints and knuckles of the fingers—similar to the practice, still found among certain European peasants, of using finger positions for multiplication. Guido taught sightsinging by letting the students associate each step of the scale with a well-known melody. This method, in the opinion of many good teachers, remains effective for the mastery of intervals even in modern music. Guido, for didactic reasons, chose a hymn of which each line begins one tone higher than the preceding line, and of which the text is obviously a singer's prayer for the cure of hoarseness: "*Ut* queant laxis/*Re*sonare fibris/*Mi*ra gestorum/*Fa*muli tuorum/*Sol*ve polluti/*La*bii reatum/*S*ancte *I*ohannes" ("That with relaxed vocal chords thy servants may be able to sing the wonders of thy deeds, remove the fault from their polluted lips, O holy John"). The association of the first syllable of each short phrase with the corresponding tone has become so permanent that, introduced as a musical game in Arezzo a thousand years ago, it has supplied the lasting nomenclature for the steps of our scale. But Guido's proudest achievement is the invention of our modern music staff. The notation of music had been effected, of course, in various ways before Guido. The old Greeks, for instance, used mainly letters of the alphabet to designate pitches. It was Guido's idea to draw horizontal lines a third apart, with special clefs to identify the pitches on and between the lines; and this idea has not been improved upon to this day.

Guido's influence was so decisive that, not only were music books and legends spuriously attributed to him throughout the Middle Ages, but also trips to Germany, France, and England. Although it is doubtful that his foot ever touched these countries, his spirit has.

ASSISI

THE SPIRITUAL POWER of the rich youth from town who became a saint is attested by the gigantic basilica of San Francesco. His poetic power, or at least the opening of his hymn to "Brother Sun," is certified by hundreds of tiles and embroideries in the little shops near the basilica. The traveler is right to suspect that a musical power has radiated from the saint as well. He was born in a society aware of strong tensions between the Church and the people. In its search for a personalized pious expression, the people accepted the new Order of St. Francis as gladly as the special song literature which he initiated. The Italian *laude,* of which the "Hymn to the Sun" is an early example, are religious songs of a popular rather than liturgical nature. The words are accordingly usually in Italian rather than Latin, and the music is simple and singable rather than technically complex.

The musical and poetic force of the *laude* caught the whole country. St. Francis had encouraged artistic activities outside the prescribed service. Within a century after his death, *compagnie de' laudesi,* clubs formed for the express purpose of singing hymns after his model and in his spirit, existed in almost every larger town—nine in Florence alone. The members, usually laborers and craftsmen from the lower social strata, would assemble in a church once a week, most often on Saturday, and find a religious outlet in "community singing." Occasionally the musical *compagnia* sang *laude* at the unveiling of a sacred image or during a procession through the streets; but there were no sermons, only songs and poetry. The *laude* literature comprises thousands of numbers. It exhausted itself about four hundred years after St. Francis set the example in Assisi.

The Franciscan Order, like the Benedictine, always considered the practice of music as an *opus Dei,* something done for God. Their most famous theological quarrel with St. Thomas Aquinas in the thirteenth century reminds one of how ascetically their Dominican opponent wanted music treated in the church. St. Francis, by contrast, encouraged gay singing to such an extent that he appealed to his brothers in this sense as *joculatores Dei,* "entertainers of God." He also subscribed to the rules of the older orders of St. Augustine and St. Benedict that church music should be sung not only with the voice but with the heart: "Cantus ecclesiastici cantentur non solum voce sed etiam corde." In a letter to the general chapter, he admonished the officiating clerics to relate the melody of the voice to the consonance of the mind: as the voice harmonizes with the mind, so the mind will harmonize with God. The positive musical spirit of the Franciscans was quickly recognized by Rome; for within half a century after the sainted founder's death, Pope Nicholas III replaced the choral books in old notation with the new Franciscan editions in modern notes.

St. Francis' deliberate adherence to the pure vocal tradition of the Roman liturgy can still be sensed by anyone attending a service in the lower church in Assisi. Although one will occasionally hear the organ, which was added to the building after 1600 under outside cultural pressures, one might also encounter a rare untainted rendition of plainchant, the unaccompanied liturgical music of the Roman Catholic Church. There is usually no service when the bus between Florence and Rome makes its thirty-minute tourist stop in the middle of the day. The traveler staying overnight in Assisi cannot spend his early morning hours more profitably than by attending a service in the lower church. Information about the exact hours and the extent of the music is easily obtained from any friar. There are often more singers participating in the service than there are members in the congregation around the traveler. On Sundays and holidays, in particular, the sensuality of the music is matched by the magnificence of the robes and the almost operatic setting, the candles behind the big iron gate dimly illuminating the frescoes by Martini and Cimabue.

BERGAMO

AT THE CLOSE of the wedding festivities in *A Midsummer Night's Dream,* a bergomask is danced for the amusement of the spectators. The fact that Bottom takes the responsibility for what Shakespeare then calls "a dance of clowns" gives a comic if not rustic coloring to the popularity of Bergamo. The *bergamasca* was danced and sung by the peasants of this town at the border of the Alps while Columbus was looking for India. To a lively melody in even beats and a dialect text, a man *in avanti* (moving forward) pursues a woman *all'indietro* (moving backward). At a change of the tune, they embrace and twirl together. By the time Shakespeare mentioned the bergomask, all Europe was dancing it without ever quite forgetting its low-class origin. As so often happens, however, the popularity of a dance results in its stylization in the hands of serious composers; and just as one finds minuets in the works of Haydn and Beethoven, and polonaises in those of Bach and Chopin, the *bergamasca* invaded the instrumental works of Frescobaldi and Scheidt (to mention only the outstanding composers of the seventeenth century), the ballets of the Vienna court, and even the last of Bach's esoteric "Goldberg" Variations. Bottom offering a bergomask was thinking as little of a town in northern Italy as a French nightclub star dancing a Charleston in the 1920's was likely to think of a town in South Carolina. Nor is it clear what Debussy had in mind when writing his *Suite Bergamasque* (of which *Clair de Lune* is a part). The modern inquisitive visitor to Bergamo, however, should be no less sensitive than the eighteenth-century musical tourist Charles Burney, who remembered upon arrival that Harlequin in the Italian Comedy at Paris always says he comes from Bergamo. In the tradition of the *commedia dell'arte,* Italian comedians used the Bergamasque dialect in Paris, because, until the reign of Louis XV, none of the buffoons was allowed to speak French.

Dr. Charles Burney published a journal of the tour through various European countries which he had undertaken in 1770 and 1772 to collect materials for a general history of music. In Bergamo, the English musician "found the houses very high; but there seems in Italian Architecture as much the taste and harmony of proportion as in their Music: every pillar we see, every gateway, portico, and colonade, has something light and graceful in it. The beauty of the windows is spoilt in the eyes of an Englishman for want of glass which we are apt to ascribe to poverty; but in all hot climates whether the inhabitants are rich or poor, paper in the windows is preferred to glass, which by reflecting the solar rays renders the heat intolerable.

"Bergamo is a large fine city . . . the upper part of which resembles Clifton near Bristol."

Burney says nothing about the basilica of Santa Maria Maggiore; and yet it has given musical direction and vitality to the whole town for many centuries, in a peculiarly centralized and yet successfully radiating manner. Around 1450 the civic leaders of the church decided to teach not only reading and writing to the clerics, charitably selected from the city's poor, but to give them music lessons in voice and instruments as well. As a result, the musical establishment of the basilica remained well supplied with local performers. The excellence of the organs consumed a great deal of intelligent attention (of which little has descended to the instruments visible and audible today). An early organ is documented in 1402, and the increased musical activity called for a new instrument in 1455. One century later, the great Graziadio Antegnati was called from Brescia to Santa Maria Maggiore. All that is left of his work are the two handsomely carved, empty cases hanging at each end of the transept and serving as picture frames for the "Birth of Christ" by Cavagna, 1593, and the "Adoration of the Magi" by Il Salmezza, 1595.

At the time the Antegnati organs were installed in 1566, the music instruction took the form and organization of a *collegio*. A double choir with the steady employment of at least forty voices and a healthy number of wind and stringed instruments placed the church music of Santa Maria Maggiore among the most respected in Europe. Much credit must go to the local sympathy for music. When the organist around the year 1500, a Frater Elia, acted in a manner most inappropriate to a public—let alone an ecclesiastic—official, he was retained in his post, after due deliberation by the church authorities, because of his extraordinary musical qualifications. One can understand the attraction of Bergamo and the music in the basilica for a man like Gafori, before the Duomo in Milan captured him for good. The long list of church musicians includes the names of the native composers Tarquinio Merula, Antonio Scandelli, and Giovanni Legrenzi; but Bergamo also exported Pietro Locatelli to Amsterdam, and Antonio Lolli to the court of Catherine the Great in St. Petersburg (where he dedicated several compositions to Prince Potëmkin).

It was a music director at Santa Maria Maggiore who lent to the historic shift of musical attention from church to theater both the quality of a long tradition and the dignity of a strong conviction. When Simon Mayr was called to Bergamo in 1802, he was thirty-nine years old. He was a native Bavarian, but the signal placement of a huge monument on his tomb in the church of Santa Maria Maggiore expresses appropriately the indebtedness of Bergamo to this foreigner (". . . pio benefico amatissimo . . . che in questa sua patria adottiva educò all'armonia cultori eminenti . . ."). He had studied in Bergamo as a youngster and made Italy his adopted home. Commissioned to write an opera for the 1794 carnival season at the Teatro La Fenice in Venice, he tasted success which produced sixty more operas before 1824. They were performed in Paris, Berlin, Vienna, Dresden, and Munich; and tunes from his operas were whistled on the streets of most Italian towns. Rossini's verve eventually superseded, but drew on, Simon Mayr's; and in Bergamo, where the manuscripts of most of his scores are kept in the Biblioteca Civica, one is more curious than ever to hear his music revived.

Mayr's church position demanded a nonoperatic output as well, and six hundred religious compositions have been credited to him—many of them large-scale oratorios, cantatas, and Masses. He remained in Bergamo until his death in 1845, notwithstanding many temptations, among them offers from such far-flung places as London, Lisbon, and Dresden, and an invitation to become Napoleon's music director at an exorbitant salary.

In Bergamo he founded two charitable institutions for aging musicians and their widows and orphans. He became the guiding spirit of the new opera house, the Teatro della Società dei Nobili Signori. He organized a chamber-music society, the Unione Filarmonica, where, playing the viola himself, he introduced the quartets of Haydn and Beethoven. For the popularization of Haydn, he also published a short biography. He shaped the music school of the basilica into a conservatory where poor boys of the community could receive a free music education. There he taught composition. Among the first dozen students admitted to the school was the nine-year-old son of an indigent family; today the Civico Istituto Musicale Gaetano Donizetti bears his name.

Whatever the genius of this best-known of all Bergamo composers, he owes a great deal to his solid early training under Simon Mayr. There is a touching reminder on the house, Via Arena No. 18 (behind the church) where he took his charity lessons from 1806 until 1815. Still in his teens, he appeared in Bergamo as a pianist and as a bass buffo singer. He played the viola in his own string quartets and he tried his hand at sacred music. He already showed his fantastic speed at composing by noting on the score of an early sinfonia: "Fatta in un'ora e un quarto." At the end of his life he needed ten weeks (some say ten days) for all of *Don Pasquale*. In between lay about seventy operas, but their successes and his enormous recognition across Europe kept him away from home, mostly in Naples and later in Paris and Vienna. Yet he felt strongly about contemporary Italian composers, writing a magnificent Requiem Mass under the impact of Bellini's death and conducting in Bologna, on a special trip from Paris, the first performance in Italy of Rossini's *Stabat Mater* in the presence of the composer. The peasantry nonsense in *L'Elisir d'Amore* may owe much of its indigenous and real charm to the traditional Bergamasque spirit. The madness of Lucia di Lammermoor is related to a deeply rooted personal disturbance. At the age of fifty, Donizetti returned to his native town in an advanced stage of insanity, and here (at what is now called the Via di Gaetano Donizetti No. 1) he died in a friend's home. His name graces the new theater in the Lower Town, the cool street behind the Duomo, and the opera stages of the whole world. He is buried near his teacher in the church of Santa Maria Maggiore.

The Istituto Musicale, on the Via Arena No. 9, contains an intimate Donizetti museum. The many Ponchielli items remind one that this composer from Cremona taught here for the last four years of his life, from 1882 to 1886. During the same period he held the position of choirmaster at the church of Santa Maria Maggiore. A plaque to the left of the choir makes it quite clear that in Bergamo he is remembered and honored, not for *Gioconda,* but for having followed the glorious footsteps of Mayr.

BOLOGNA

CITIES, LIKE PEOPLE, have certain characteristics. They can even be musical in different ways. Cremona is known for violinmakers, and Naples for opera. Bologna is the seat of an old university which has impregnated with a scholarly spirit the air of more than the classrooms. The composers and performers of Bologna, who could not complain of a shortage of churches and theaters, appear insignificant compared to the eminent scholars and teachers who have determined the town's musical character for centuries.

The university was founded in the eleventh century. When Dante and Petrarch attended it in the second half of the thirteenth century, they belonged to a student population of ten thousand. The ease that foreign students have felt in Bologna all through the centuries was legally established in the twelfth century by the Emperor Frederick Barbarossa, who granted them special immunities and privileges, particularly protection against the landlords in whose houses they were domiciled.

The chair of music at the university was first sanctioned by a Papal bull of 1450. Many of the music professors in Bologna were great men, among them Bartolomeo Ramos de Pareja and Giovanni Maria Artusi. It was the latter who called Monteverdi's imaginative innovations "imperfections of modern music." He thereby displayed a conservative attitude that seems to be a concomitant of academic eminence in Bologna as elsewhere. Torquato Tasso, a student in 1564, was tried for writing a satirical poem; and Richard Wagner, three hundred years later, showed his respect for the judiciary role of the city by endeavoring to find acceptance for his music dramas there as a passport to subsequent Italian successes.

On 21 August 1770, an English tourist, who had recently received his D.Mus. at Oxford, stood fearfully at the Bologna customhouse "on account of books," he records in his journal, "which I had been told were always sent to the inquisition to be examined. But no such thing happened to mine." His chief business in this city was "to see and converse with the learned Padre Martini . . . regarded by all Europe as the deepest theorist." Before Dr. Charles Burney left ten days later, he had come to admire the library of seventeen thousand volumes belonging to the most eminent music professor of the century. Nor was he the only musician that week who had journeyed to Bologna for the special purpose of securing the judgment and blessing of the wise Franciscan priest, the music professor Giovanni Battista Martini. On 30 August, Burney writes: "I had been desired by P. Martini to attend to the performances at the Church of S. Giovanni in Monte, where he did not choose to go himself, the members of the Philharmonic society being chiefly, if not all, his disciples; and said he wished to have the opinion of an unprejudiced professor, an utter stranger to them all. . . . There was a great deal of Company. . . . and among the rest, who should I meet but the celebrated little German, Mozart, who in 1766 astonished all hearers in London by his premature musical talent. I had a long conversation with his father. . . . The little man is grown considerably but is still a little man. . . . There is no musical excellence which I do not expect from his extraordinary quickness and talents, under the guidance of so able a musician and intelligent man as his father . . ."

Burney left for Florence the next day ("I cannot quit this city without returning once more to the good Padre Martini. . . . We parted, on my side with sorrow"). The Mozarts, father and son, stayed for another six weeks to secure the final stamp of approval of the Bologna musical tribunal for the fourteen-year-old boy: membership in the Accademia Filarmonica.

There are several aspects to the story of Wolfgang's admission. The proud father wrote to his wife, who had stayed in Salzburg: "On 9 October Wolfgang had to appear in the hall of the Academy at four o'clock in the afternoon. There . . . three old Kapellmeisters put before him, in the presence of all the members, an antiphon taken out of an antiphonario, which he had to arrange for four parts in an anteroom, into which the beadle led him, locking the door behind him. When Wolfgang had finished it, it was examined by the Censores and all the Kapellmeisters and Compositores. Then a vote was taken, which was done by means of white and black balls. As all the balls were white, Wolfgang was called in and all the members clapped their hands as he entered and congratulated him, and the Princeps of the Academy informed him, on behalf of the company, that he had passed the examination. He thanked them and then the ceremony was over. . . . All the members were surprised that Wolfgang had finished his task so quickly, seeing that many candidates had spent three hours over an antiphon of three lines. For I must tell you that it is not at all an easy task . . . This distinction does Wolfgang all the more credit as the Accademia Bonnoniensis is more than a hundred years old and, apart from Padre Martini and other eminent Italians, only the most distinguished citizens of other countries are members of it."

Actually Wolfgang Amadeus Mozart did not do very well in the examination. In the library of the Conservatorio di Musica G. B. Martini on the Piazza Rossini, his original exercise can be seen as he completed it in seclusion. It is full of corrections made by Padre Martini, whose status in the Accademia permitted him to be helpful and friendly to the immature candidate. The official verdict was a low passing mark: "At the end of less than an hour Signor Mozart brought his essay and in view of the special circumstances it was adjudged sufficient." ("Nel termine di meno d'un'ora ha esso Sr. Mozart portato il suo esperimento, il quale riguardo alle circostanze di esso lui è giudicato sufficiente.") The truth as veiled by Leopold Mozart increases the stature of Padre Martini and of the Accademia without in the least diminishing that of the prodigious Salzburg composer. Instead of adhering to a rigid interpretation of the academic standards, the Bolognese savants trusted their instincts and, by considering Mozart a good risk, forever associated themselves with musical genius.

The Conservatorio, formerly the Liceo, is rightly named after G. B. Martini, as much for his preeminence among music educators as for the priceless library it inherited from him. As recently as 1961, the size and importance of his book collection was recognized by a reissue of the catalogue, which alone fills four volumes. Padre Martini was gratified by his awareness that without leaving his cell, or at least Bologna, he could converse and deal with many masters of old and new times, not only with Spaniards and Romans, but also with English, Greek, French, and German composers and theorists. The Liceo Filarmonico, continuing a long tradition of music instruction, was organized in 1804 when the political upheaval in Napoleon's maelstrom necessitated a parallel reappraisal of social and artistic conditions. The monastery of San Giacomo had become vacant as the result of the French destruction and dispersion of religious orders. The new music school intended, and eventually somehow managed, to direct the various musical currents into one stream. An early power struggle between the venerable Accademia Filarmonica and the upstart Liceo invoked futile legal intervention by the city and even by the Pope, until the appointment of Rossini in 1839 as *consulente perpetuo* and his brilliant administration for nine years laid the foundation on which the school has built its lasting renown. The composer of *Guillaume Tell* was then middle-aged, and his unique prestige and keen mind permitted him to shape both faculty and curriculum freely and harmoniously. A plaque near the entrance door recalls his connection with the conservatory first as a student and then as director.

The association of a church with a music school, incidental in the case of San Giacomo and the Conservatorio G. B. Martini, is often traditional and planned. The church of San Petronio has trained seemingly endless generations of musicians, and its location on the Piazza Maggiore is a physical expression of its central position in the music life of Bologna. Of the two organs in San Petronio, the one on the right choir loft is one of the few fifteenth-century organs of which the original sound and mechanics are almost entirely intact. It was played when Charles V, on 24 February 1530, was crowned by the same Pope Clement VII whose city he had sacked three years earlier. The scene, without the organ, was painted by Vasari for the huge council room of the Palazzo Vecchio in Florence as a vindication, no doubt, of the Medici Pope. The populace in the piazza outside the church feasted on two bullocks roasted whole and on wine pouring from the fountains, while silver was freely scattered everywhere. The emperor was almost killed by the accidental fall of some scaffolding. The organ has miraculously survived. It was built in 1470 by Lorenzo Ugolini di Giacomo, of Prato. The old Gothic case has been largely covered by Baroque stucco, but it remains recognizable, particularly on the side of the rear *prospectus* with its old painted decorations. The twelve registers, on a low wind pressure of forty-two millimeters, fill the huge church with life and beauty. The diapason choir, in particular, once heard, remains unforgettable. The qualified visitor applying in the sacristy (to the right of the choir) might get permission to play the organ himself. From the loft, he will find an easy access into the instrument; and a walk among the old pipes, spring chests, and iron trackers is worth the dust on one's trousers.

By the time the second organ, on the left choir, was added in 1596 (an excellent instrument in its own right), the church had begun to serve God with the assistance of an orchestra. The Bolognese pleasure in sensual opulence can be gratified by violins, violas, and trombones as well as by wines, sausages, and chicken. In San Petronio the lush sound of an orchestra soon matched the rich decorations of the architecture. This was the home of the Bologna school of instrumental music. In the second half of the seventeenth century, Vitali and Torelli emerged from the church orchestra not only as supreme performers on the modern stringed instruments but as founders of the modern type of the concerto. They gave form and life to the Baroque *concerto grosso* (of which Bach's "Brandenburg" Concertos, for instance, supply well-known late examples), and Torelli is credited with the composition of the first solo concerto for violin and orchestra. It was violin instruction that attracted the teen-aged Corelli to Bologna, and he repaid his indebtedness by identifying himself as "Bolognese" on his first three publications. The ingenious sonority of his sonatas and concertos for strings represents in everlasting and popular freshness the wealth radiating from San Petronio.

If the Bolognese expected sensual satisfaction in a church, they certainly were in need of a theater. The Teatro Comunale, a few blocks beyond the conservatory, embodies the secular aspirations of the city's musical splendor. The Galli-Bibiena family was at home in Bologna and in theater construction.

Eight members of the family, spanning the late Baroque of the seventeenth and eighteenth centuries in four generations, brought to an utmost technical refinement the art of building theaters and scenic decorations. The emperors in Vienna employed them heavily, but it would be difficult to find a court in Europe without the traces of at least one Galli-Bibiena. This is not the moment to draw distinctions among the different family members. The architect of the Teatro Comunale in Bologna belonged to the third generation; his life filled a major part of the eighteenth century. His sense for stage sets can be cherished in Bologna in his *trompe l'œil* paintings in the churches of Santa Maria della Vita and San Procolo (neither one far from the Piazza Maggiore). He is the same Antonio Galli-Bibiena whose Teatro Scientifico in Mantua aroused the admiration of the Mozarts on their first trip to Italy.

The spacious Bologna opera house was opened on 14 May 1763 with a performance of *Il Trionfo di Clelia* by Gluck on a text by Metastasio. This was the year after the novel and impressive *Orfeo ed Euridice* in Vienna. Gluck asked the young Dittersdorf to accompany him on the long journey, and the violinist's autobiography records many details of the trip. He told Gluck sadly: " 'I have not the money to do so.' 'Ah,' Gluck answered, cold and alienated. 'In that case, of course, nothing can come of the matter.' " Friends contributed the money anyhow, and the two musicians enjoyed themselves in Bologna. The opera singers gave a benefit concert for Gluck, who was fond of money. He was also fond of food and parties, which absorbed more of his day than the few morning hours reserved for the completion of the opera. Padre Martini was duly visited. There were seventeen full rehearsals. If the composer and his friend Dittersdorf were not satisfied with the performance, putting most of the blame on the imprecise Italian orchestra, the Bolognese were even less so. The intake from twenty-eight performances did not cover the deficit, which had been underwritten by fifty-six public-minded guarantors, and the following dialect ditty accompanied Gluck's return trip:

Dman al part al Cluch
El va per Triest;
Ch'al faga ben prest,
Perchè l'è un gran Mameluch.

(Tomorrow departs Gluck,
He goes by way of Trieste;
Let him be quick about it,
For he is a great Mameluke.)

Il Trionfo di Clelia has not been heard since, anywhere. This tepid inauguration could not diminish the architectural glamour, but the musical history of the Teatro Comunale has never lived up to its physical possibilities. Thus Wagner's first introduction to Italy by a *Lohengrin* production in 1871 remains the most noteworthy event; and bronze reliefs of both Wagner and Verdi dominate the entrance hall. The title role at this performance, Americans might care to know, was sung by the same Italo Campanini from Parma who twelve years later as Faust opened the new Metropolitan Opera House in New York. Visitors outside the season will enjoy a glimpse of the hall by gaining admission through the stage door on the left flank of the building.

BRESCIA

THE CHURCH OF San Giuseppe is not even mentioned in several of the currently popular and reputable guidebooks. Yet it houses what experts agree is the best organ in Italy. (The best Italian organ is in Austria, in the Silver Chapel of the Imperial Palace at Innsbruck—an unsurpassed and perfectly preserved *organo di legno* built in Italy just before the middle of the sixteenth century.) The instrument in San Giuseppe dates back to the period when the church was just being completed. From an inscription, handsomely carved just below the front pipes, we learn that Gratiadeus Antegnatus, a citizen of Brescia, made the organ in 1581. He was a member of a family which, from the fifteenth to the seventeenth centuries, dominated organ construction in northern Italy with superior knowledge, craft, and taste. The many instruments the Antegnatis delivered to the cathedrals in Milan, Mantua, Bergamo, Como, and Venice, and to churches of other towns, are today little more than make-believe, handsome but empty shells filled with inferior pipes of later periods. The organ in Brescia is almost intact and renders the closest realization in Italy today of the sound ideal of the *cinquecento*.

The pipes are all of almost pure lead. Of the thirteen stops, the *flauto in ottava* and the pedal were added subsequently; but the entire diapason pyramid has the breath and life of the original. The glorious sound—mystic yet clear, effortless yet strong—is aided by the marvelous acoustics of the church. The visual impression corresponds to the aural. Suspended between two columns, the organ looks noble and a bit austere, depending for decoration on restrained painting rather than on sumptuous architecture. There is nothing superfluous about it.

Graziadio's son Costanzo probably assisted in the construction. Beside following his father's profession, he also established himself as the church organist and as a composer. His tombstone in the second chapel of the left aisle originally delineated an organ; but the iconoclasts of 1797 destroyed the carved image, mistaking it for an aristocratic escutcheon.

Costanzo knew the value of tradition. He had before him the organ in the Duomo Vecchio built by his granduncle Gian Giacomo Antegnati in 1536, and he did not hesitate to call it one of the best in the world. The long line of organ-building Antegnatis in Brescia has been rightly compared to the analogous tradition of the Amatis, Stradivaris, and Guarneris only thirty miles away in Cremona. What is there in this small geographic circumference that has produced the most preeminent instrument builders in European history? They all were highly educated and intelligent, and they practiced their craft not just as a commercial profession but as an inspired art. They reached perfection by concentrating on essentials.

The church of San Giuseppe is approached from the Piazza della Loggia by a street named for Gasparo da Salò; and if his popular identification as "the inventor of the modern violin" is a well-meant legendary exaggeration, his role as one of the creators of the present form and brilliance of the violin has made Brescia famous the world over. Here he was active most of his life, less than twenty miles away from his native Salò on Lake Garda. The Cremona masters who followed were all indebted to him. Coming to Brescia in his twenties, however, he was on the point of abandoning the musical profession of his father and grandfather and emigrating to France when the timely loan of sixty lire by a monk, Brother Gabriel of St. Piero, encouraged him to pursue his career as *artefice de instrumenti de musicha.* He opened his first shop in the Contrada del Palazzo Vecchio (now the Via Dante); later he owned houses in the Contrada delle Cossere and the Vicolo S. Pietro Martire. Although his houses are no longer standing, a walk through the old quarter behind the Loggia quickly reveals that the form and flavor of the little streets have been preserved. Gasparo da Salò's most elaborate violin was commissioned by Cardinal Aldobrandini, who gave it as a present to the Innsbruck treasury. Appropriated by Napoleon's army in 1809, it was eventually purchased by the Norwegian virtuoso Ole Bull. The head of this violin, the face of an angel, was allegedly carved by Benvenuto Cellini; the tailpiece is a bronze-colored mermaid; there are blue and gold inlays on the fingerboard; and the bridge is delicately carved in the zodiacal image of the two intertwining fish. None of these eccentricities diminishes, or for that matter enhances, the inherent musical beauty of the violin, which can be seen behind glass in the Vestlandske Kunstindustrimuseum in Bergen, Norway (the leading English and German encyclopedias have confused this violin with another Gasparo da Salò owned by Ole Bull when suggesting that it found its way to America). Gasparo da Salò was buried in San Giuseppe in 1609; his tombstone having disappeared, a tablet outside the church notes the fact.

The same church, which seems to hold the musical memorabilia of the town, also covers the remains of Benedetto Marcello. His imprint on Venice is known to the traveler; he died in Brescia in 1739 while on a political mission. His splendid tombstone toward the front of the middle aisle renders him due honor.

Marcello probably attended the Teatro Grande, which

has stood since 1710 in the center of town, and the traveler today should follow his example. (The custodian can be found at the back of the building in the narrow Via Paganora No. 19a.) In the eighteenth century, the audience was impressed by its splendor, spaciousness, and modern comforts; and the visitor today ascends the same open staircase into the fantastic rococo *ridotto* (now the lobby and bar) that enchanted the crowd of 1782. The opening of the big auditorium in 1811 was punctuated by a new opera, *Sacrificio di Ifigenia,* by Simon Mayr, then at home in Bergamo and popular throughout Europe. The excellent proportions and acoustics of the wooden hall have not been harmed by the lavish stucco and the gilded decorations added in the 1860's. The elegance of the house is emphasized by a row of little parlors: a *retropalco* is assigned to, but separated by a corridor from, each box. The boxholders own and manage the Teatro Grande as a co-operative social venture. In this auditorium (with Arrigo Boito in the crowd), Puccini's *Madama Butterfly* was rehabilitated in 1904 a few months after the notorious initial fiasco in Milan.

BUSSETO

A PILGRIMAGE TO the birthplace of a great man is rewarding to anyone curious about the spirit of a place, i.e., to a tourist ideally defined. A visit to Busseto is doubly rewarding; for Giuseppe Verdi both was born in this region and chose it as a homestead for the second half of his long life.

Busseto lies about fifteen miles south of Cremona on the spur track to Fidenza, and a little over twenty miles away from Parma, the capital of the province. A car, or at least a taxi rented in Busseto, seems indispensable for tracing the Verdi landmarks, which are about six miles apart in opposite directions from the center of town.

Le Roncole is a little hamlet within the township of Busseto. The house in which the composer was born is now a national monument. In 1813 the solid but poor building was the village inn and village shop in which Carlo Verdi, innkeeper and grocer, toiled as hard as the dusty and parched peasants he served. One year after Giuseppe was born, the defeat of Napoleon brought the victorious allied armies to northern Italy. The aim of the invaders was to turn out the occupation forces of the French; but the Russian and Austrian soldiers passing through Le Roncole indiscriminately murdered even those inhabitants who had gathered in the asylum of the church. They did not stretch their brutal pursuit up into the belfry where the Verdi family was hiding.

The church still stands and permits one to imagine not

only the infant in the tower but also the growing child at the organ. At twelve, he was the village organist, succeeding his teacher in office. He continued to play the organ in Le Roncole every Sunday and holiday even after moving to Busseto to attend the nearest school. The traveler today is not likely to walk the three miles from Busseto to Le Roncole. One Christmas morning before daybreak, the boy Verdi fell off the winding road into the adjoining ditch and was saved from drowning by a chance passer-by. "I had a hard time as a boy," he told his biographer Bellaigue in his old age. But he also had a piano which his understanding father had found for him and to which Verdi felt so indebted that he kept it all his life. Today it is under glass in the Museo Teatrale alla Scala in Milan. It looks primitive enough, but inside is the report of a friendly neighbor who turned the broken-down spinet into a usable instrument: "These hammers were repaired and recovered with leather by me, Stefano Cavaletti, and I fitted the pedals which I gave as a present; I also repaired the said hammers without charge, noting the good disposition the young Verdi has for learning to play this instrument, which is sufficient for my complete satisfaction—Anno Domini 1821." While in Le Roncole, let us think kindly and gratefully of the local peasant Cavaletti, for our complete satisfaction.

The Verdi house looks genuine and strong. The father's osteria now lodges the custodian. The vaulted store to the left of the entrance shows its former structure. The well in the yard yields water for flowers. In the guest book, homage has been paid to the house by the autographs of public figures (including a king, a cardinal, and a dictator), of musicians (including the leading composers, singers, and conductors of recent generations), and of thousands of travelers from all corners of the earth. (We might as well mention that the sophisticated coffeehouse next door is not only a convenience for the traveler but also part of the home of the creator of Don Camillo, Giovanni Guareschi, who lives upstairs.)

Compared to Le Roncole, Busseto is a metropolis with a touch of elegance propagated over the centuries by the Pallavicino family. Carlo Verdi bought his wine and groceries from the wealthy merchant Antonio Barezzi, and in 1826 he sent him his son to gather experience and education. Barezzi loved music. He could play the highest and the lowest instruments, the flute and the ophicleide, in the local Philharmonic Society, which met in his house and of which he was the president. His daughter Margherita played duets with the boy (and married him ten years later). Eventually Verdi conducted the community orchestra and the town band, for which he also wrote some compositions.

Barezzi's status in Busseto is represented by the location of his house on the central piazza (now named after the boy he took in), where it squarely faces the dominating Pallavicino castle. The community has put a commemorative tablet on the house and made a post office of Barezzi's old store. But the painted decorations inside the doorway are those Verdi saw, and the ornamented initial *B* on the ceiling radiates a personal intimacy.

A picture of Barezzi and of those early years in Busseto emerges from a letter sent by Verdi to a friend four decades later: "You know I owe everything to him, everything, everything. And to him alone, not to other people, as they've tried to make out. I can still see him (and this was many years ago), when I had finished school in Busseto, and my father declared he couldn't support me at the University of Parma, and I had just decided to go back to the village where I was born.

"When the good old man found it out, he said to me: 'You were sent into the world for something better than to sell salt and work as a farmer. Ask the Monte di Pietà for the little stipend of 25 francs a month for four years, and I'll undertake the rest. You shall go to the Conservatory of Milan and shall pay me back the money I've spent for you when you're able.'

"And so it was! You see, he was a generous, good, loving man. I've met all kinds of men, but never a better one! He loved me as much as his own son, and I loved him like a father."

Barezzi felt amply repaid by Verdi's career. Less than two weeks after he had traveled to Florence for the first *Macbeth* performance in 1847 and had witnessed thirty-eight curtain calls for the composer, he received the following letter:

"I have long intended to dedicate an opera to you, who have been father, benefactor, and friend to me. It was a duty I should have fulfilled sooner if imperious circumstances had not prevented me. Now I send you *Macbeth,* which I prize above all my other operas and therefore consider most worthy to present to you. My heart offers it: may the heart receive it! It is a testimony of my eternal gratitude and love for you.—G. Verdi."

Verdi's affection attached itself to the whole landscape. He expressed his faith in the European revolution of 1848 by buying a house and surrounding farmlands near Busseto. Sant'Agata was his home for the next half century until his death in 1901. The tiny village, three miles outside Busseto, actually belongs to the province of Piacenza, but Verdi was not the man to let the little brook Ungine in front of his estate dictate his allegiance. The visitor to the villa learns a great deal about the composer, for Verdi spent much personal energy in remodeling the house and planting the gardens. The shady groves are all his work, and a huge betula tree is pointed out as the only one on his land that preceded him. He must have waited with patience and faith for the planned natural protection from the summer heat of the flat, fertile farmland. The happy release of energy made possible by the quiet and familiar countryside found its reverberation in the quick completion of *Rigoletto, Il Trovatore,* and *La Traviata* within the first three years after he moved to Sant'Agata.

The house looks today as it did when he lived in it. The upper story is occupied by his heirs. The rooms of the composer and his second wife, the beautiful singer Giuseppina Strepponi, have remained touchingly personal. On a bookshelf next to his bed one notes fifteen little volumes of chamber music by Haydn, Mozart, and Beethoven, next to the writings of Schiller, Shakespeare, and Dante. On a piece of paper, now under glass, Verdi wrote: "Un Tedesco che sa, sa troppo. Un Russo che sa è un pericolo." ("A German who knows, knows too much. A Russian who knows is a danger.") The main library in the adjoining room safeguards his manuscripts. One senses the man's genuine tastes and interests from the collection on the shelves. Among an abundance of nineteenth-century opera scores, Wagner is not neglected.

In 1857 Busseto considered the construction of a theater. Verdi's reaction was typical: "Italy is in great danger . . . from her lack of money . . . Busseto is building a theater. Don't think I condemn this plan, even if it be vain and useless as it seems to me . . . We must consider higher and more important matters. And so I am asking the town council to suspend this work . . . and to employ the money for our country's finances." Yet the theater became a reality in 1869. Built into the right wing of the Rocca dei Marchesi Pallavicino, the castle on the central square, it is well worth a visit. Here Toscanini conducted *Falstaff* in 1913 on the centennial of Verdi's birth in order to raise funds for a monument; and he repeated the same opera with his legendary ensemble from La Scala in 1926 on the twenty-fifth anniversary of the composer's death. One envies the six hundred listeners who could hear either performance in such personal and intimate surroundings.

CATANIA

THIS CITY HAS done a great deal to honor the memory of her native son, the opera composer Vincenzo Bellini. The handsome and huge public gardens (in the northern part of the city) are named after him. So is the lush *fin-de-siècle* opera house and the square in front of it. His statue in the central Piazza Stesicoro fills a large area. It is surrounded by figures from his most famous operas: *Norma, I Puritani, Il Pirata,* and *La Sonnambula.* Even on picture postcards, Bellini themes vie with the famous Catania elephant for popularity. Yet there is irony in the fact that little connects Bellini with Catania beside the accident of his birth—a contrast to the neglect many musicians have suffered after spending a whole life in a community.

Bellini's family stemmed from the Abruzzi, which the composer's grandfather had left in the 1760's for professional reasons. He was a good musician and eventually was appointed choir director at the cathedral in Catania, a position that his son inherited from him. The grandson Vincenzo was born in 1801 in the house still standing in the Piazza Francesco d'Assisi No. 3 (on the way from the cathedral to the Greek theater). The rooms now contain a small Bellini museum and deserve a visit.

Vincenzo Bellini studied music with his grandfather, but also received a good humanistic education, for which the Greek and Roman ruins at the foot of his house may have aroused an early interest. In the palaces of the local aristocracy he was exposed in his early teens to the chamber music of Haydn and Mozart. His musical talent soon became apparent, and at eighteen he was sent to study at the conservatory in Naples. He returned to Catania only once during his lifetime, in early 1832, after his operatic successes elsewhere—notably in Naples, Venice, and Milan—assured him of a triumphant reception. By that time he had already written *Il Pirata* for the Teatro alla Scala, the plot of which deals with an episode from Sicily's history. Then he left for new personal and musical conquests that carried him as far as London. He died not quite thirty-four years old in a suburb of Paris where he had hoped to settle. His body was returned to Catania forty-one years later and was put to rest in the cathedral, near the second pier on the right.

The melodic power and beauty of his operas have been deeply admired by composers as different from each other as Wagner and Verdi. The former, in a special essay dedicated to Bellini whose *Norma* he had chosen for his benefit performance at the Riga theater in 1837, wrote: "Here, where the poem itself soars up to the tragic height of the ancient Greeks, this form [of Italian opera], pronouncedly ennobled by Bellini, does but heighten the solemn and grandiose character of the whole; all the passions which his song so distinctively transfigures thereby obtain a majestic foundation, on which they do not flutter about vaguely but shape themselves to one grand and lucid picture." Verdi, in a letter to the French music critic Camille Bellaigue, of 2 May 1898, summarized his views: "Bellini . . . is rich in feeling and in a certain personal melancholy, which is completely his own! Even in his less well-known operas like *La Straniera* and *Il Pirata,* there are long, long, long spun-out melodies, like nothing that had been written before. How powerful and true the declamation is, for example, in the duet between Pollione and Norma. And what a lofty flight of thought there is in the first phrase of the introduction to *Norma,* which is followed after a few measures by another theme . . . No one has ever written anything of more heavenly beauty."

At the time Bellini's grandfather emigrated to Catania, a musical venture of a unique kind attracted the attention of visitors and inhabitants alike. The church of San Nicolò l'Arena had been built after the earthquake of 1693, a spectacular testimony to eighteenth-century taste. It still is the largest church in Sicily. The apse is impressively filled by an organ of almost three thousand pipes distributed over three consoles, of which the one pedal and five manuals are to be played by three organists simultaneously. This predecessor of a modern American movie-house organ is musically less satisfactory than a Bellini aria; but the case and the theatrical idea are rather remarkable. Goethe considered it a tourist attraction twenty years after its installation, and he commented in the diary of his Sicilian journey on 3 May 1787 that "the skilful musician who alone could manage the enormous organ . . . in the very spacious church . . . made its softest notes whisper through its remotest corners, or filled the whole of it with the crash of its loudest tones." The church suffered severe war damage in 1943; but the organ, temporarily muted, could be repaired if anyone really cared.

CREMONA

THE TWELFTH-CENTURY CATHEDRAL is a main attraction of this town, and in the cathedral the organ deserves as much attention as the frescoes. The beautiful instrument was built around 1480 and soon became famous for its magnificent sound. It caused a significant quarrel when it had to be rebuilt about a century later (we must assume that the many invasions by foreign armies and the political insecurity of the early sixteenth century particularly in northern Italy were mostly responsible for the quick decay). The municipal organ repairman, Gian Francesco Mainero, who had been commissioned to replace deficient pipes, decided on his own to lower the pitch of the whole instrument by one half-tone. He was bitterly opposed by Marc'Antonio Ingegneri, the church organist and, incidentally, Monteverdi's teacher at the time of the quarrel (1583). After months of public hearings and committee meetings, the composer won out over the technician (as he should). The verdict spells out the concern that "l'istromento rimanesse privo di tuono, et vivacità di spirito . . . che molto è bisognevole al corpo grande della chiesa." Although our pitch today is universally a half-tone lower than it was on sixteenth-century organs (thus exonerating Mainero to a certain extent), one sympathizes with Ingegneri who worried that the organ might lose that vivacity of spirit which is desirable in a huge building like the cathedral.

Apart from the fact that Monteverdi was born here in

1567 and as a boy certainly sang in the cathedral choir, receiving good guidance by Ingegneri before leaving for Mantua, Cremona is not famous for her composers. But the city has the unique distinction of having brought forth the best stringed instruments of all times. The Amati, Guarneri, and Stradivari families all lived and worked in Cremona from about 1550 to about 1760. Craftsmanship, tradition, climate, wood—did they all conspire to produce violins that have never been surpassed or, for that matter, sufficiently explained?

Nicola Amati, of the third violin-making generation in his family, created his masterpieces while the pilgrims in New England were chopping down trees to build their first houses. His instruments are admired for their sweet and mellow tone which carries without being obtrusive. The inherent lack of aggressiveness has kept Amati violins away from the modern concert life; but an Amati viola launched the early career of William Primrose, and Leonard Rose's violoncello speaks with a rare persuasiveness. Nicola Amati was the teacher of Andrea Guarneri and Antonio Stradivari, both of them fathers and founders of long lines of violinmakers.

The Guarneri violins have a stronger "bite" than either of the other Cremonese products. Isaac Stern and Jascha Heifetz often perform on instruments built by Andrea's second cousin Guarneri del Gesù, who spent several years in jail for killing another violinmaker.

The supreme master of them all is doubtless Antonio Stradivari. The sound of his violins has radiated from Cremona to the ends of the earth. His native community was very much embarrassed to realize a few years ago that not one of his instruments was left in town. Money was collected from all sides, and in December 1961 the municipality purchased from a dealer in the United States a Stradivari violin of 1715, once the property of Joseph Joachim, for thirty million lire (fifty thousand dollars). The short-necked instrument is the pride of the city. It is kept, not in the museum as one might expect, but in the city hall, the Gothic Palazzo Comunale facing the cathedral. There it stands under glass on a marble pedestal, right next to the mayor's office and the council chamber on the top floor, in a handsome front room used for civil weddings ("which occur rarely, for a few Communists in town," the guard volunteered affably). The municipal guards beam at any visitor requesting to be conducted to the shrine, and the wise city fathers permit the violin to be played by qualified performers.

Antonio Stradivari's apartment and shop at the time of his first marriage (1667–80) were in the *casa di Messer Pescatore,* now Corso Garibaldi No. 55–57 (the shop inexplicably bears the number 1088). There is no marker on the house, but the remodeling of the bottega in 1962 caused a furor in the local paper and in the local conversation. Stradivari's earnings were high. The house which he purchased in 1680 at the age of thirty-six, which he inhabited most of his life, and in which he died in 1737 at the age of ninety-three, stood on what is now the choice spot of the modern *galleria,* Piazza Roma No. 1. The phrase *ricco come Stradivari* ("rich like Stradivari") became proverbial in his own day. In front of his house, the Dominicans had their church, and in it he was buried. This temple of the Inquisition was eventually replaced by a garden—so a pedestal surrounded by plants and flowers tells us. The place of Antonio Stradivari's tomb was preserved by the municipal council. His grave is fifty steps in front of the house he lived in, and it is now surrounded by Cremona's handsomest park and by the active life of the population. He had purchased the burial place and tombstone from the noble family Villani, whose coat of arms and family inscriptions are still visible under the Stradivari name.

It is to be expected in this town that streets have been named after Amati, Guarneri, and Stradivari. One notes without further comment that the current telephone directory lists forty-nine Guarneris and not a single Amati and Stradivari (there are six Monteverdis, for that matter, and no Ingegneri). One tourist, at least, was relieved and pleased to discover on the program of a local dance school the name of Stradivari among the female members of the *corps de ballet.*

Stradivari violins are favored by almost all leading concert violinists. Joseph Joachim used several during his career and possessed three fine specimens at the time of his death. The Library of Congress in Washington owns a whole string quartet of Stradivari instruments and permits them to be played in the building at its annual chamber-music cycles and broadcasts.

Cremona is now the seat of the Scuola Internazionale di Liuteria, located in the modern Palazzo dell'Arte, which attempts to keep the tradition alive by training, and issuing diplomas to, masters in violin-building. Attached to it is a museum, the Museo Civico di Organologia e di Storia della Musica "A. Stradivari." One reaches the building from the Stradivari house on the Piazza Roma through a succession, quite properly, of musical streets: the Corso Stradivari, the Via Verdi, and the Via Monteverdi. The museum offers a fascinating display of tools, forms, patterns, materials, models, drawings, and paper cuts used by Stradivari for the construction of scrolls, pegs, necks, bridges, violin bodies, and bows. The collection includes a handful of Amati drawings and models (none by Guarneri) and many stringed instruments by minor masters of the Cremonese school, but not the one perfect and conspicuous Stradivari violin in town.

Amidst the loving concern shown for Stradivari, Monteverdi has been rather neglected. But another composer born in Cremona has been signally honored, perhaps because *L'Incoronazione di Poppea* is removed in time and taste from the Cremonese citizen when compared with *Gioconda.* The statue of Amilcare Ponchielli graces the park near the Stradivari tomb, and the handsome Teatro Concordia of 1808 has been renamed after the composer. Although the theater has not made history (apart from one inevitable *prima assoluta* by Ponchielli, his first opera *I Promessi Sposi* in 1856), the interior is attractive enough to warrant a visit. The custodian is located in the courtyard of Corso Vittorio Emanuele No. 52, to the left of the opera house.

On his vacation trip in 1890, Johannes Brahms arrived in Cremona on Good Friday. He stayed at the Hotel Pavone at Via Solferino No. 9–15, which connects the two main squares in town. The hotel is still available to tourists, although there is no telling what the radical renovation in progress in late 1962 may have done to it. Provided Brahms could find good food and wine, he preferred unpretentious *alberghi* to luxurious establishments. Whatever his thoughts about a Mass for male choir by a local composer which he heard in the cathedral on Easter Sunday, he was most happy to discover an altar dedicated to St. Joachim (San Gioacchino) in the Lombard-Gothic church of Sant'Agostino (the third in the left aisle). Thinking of his violinist-friend in Berlin he remarked to his travel companion Widmann that it was only proper for Joachim (the greatest violinist of his generation) to have a monument in the renowned city of violins.

FERRARA

THE GENIUS LOCI of an artistic town often remains an elusive spirit. In Ferrara, nevertheless, it seems to bear the name of Este. Raising one's eyes to the wonderful campanile to the right of the cathedral or tracing the allegoric frescoes in the Palazzo Schifanoia, the traveler is in the presence of witnesses to the sensitive interests of the Este family. He will not be aware of music in the empty halls of the mansion until he is reminded that the musical grandeur of the Este court far surpassed the pictorial—regardless of how one appraises Tura and Costa. Actually, the continuous musical wealth and variety of Ferrara during the Renaissance were hardly surpassed by any other Italian community.

The musical vitality of Ferrara seemed to shrivel along with the political when the rule of the house of Este was superseded, in 1598, by that of the Holy See. But through compositions and documents of the two preceding centuries, the love for music of each of seven successive Este lords glows as freshly as the color in a luminous painting.

Characteristic of the Este rulers throughout the fourteenth and fifteenth centuries is their imaginative and careful search for the best musicians wherever they could be found. This "international" attitude is not unlike that of the Metropolitan Opera Association of New York, for instance, in the earlier decades of this century, with good results in either case. Even as early as the year 1200, the first absolute Este ruler of

Ferrara, Azzo VI, provided hospitality and admiration for the Provençal troubadour Aimeric de Péguilhan. But beginning with Niccolò III in the early *quattrocento,* the search for foreign artists became systematic, and the greatest composers of the Renaissance appeared in Ferrara.

Each period in history seems to have a particular geographic center of musical gravity. In the fifteenth century it lay in the Netherlands and at the Burgundian court. If it shifted to Italy in the sixteenth century, much credit attaches to the unceasing efforts of the house of Este to attract the best Netherlands composers to the warmer climate and to better working conditions. Niccolò III asked Philip the Good of Burgundy for musicians and instruments, and the then most powerful ruler in Europe obliged him by shipping a woodwind ensemble of four shawms, four cromornes, and four flutes. The same Niccolò III showed his friendship and appreciation for Guillaume Dufay before the Netherlands composer had become a celebrity. Dufay was in his early thirties when he dedicated a ballad, "C'est bien raison," to Niccolò. A gift of twenty gold ducats that he received from Niccolò equaled the monthly salary he then drew as a singer in the Papal chapel. Dufay lovers today may wish to acknowledge the equestrian statue of Niccolò III on the small Renaissance arch in front of the Palazzo Comunale, opposite the cathedral. Although a modern reproduction of a fifteenth-century original, the face probably looks as it did when Dufay saw it.

Among Niccolò's sons, who ruled Ferrara successively and collected musical instruments enthusiastically, Ercole I has the worst political record, for he lost some territory; and the most glorious artistic record, for he gathered around him, among others, the poet Lodovico Ariosto and the musicians Jacob Obrecht and Josquin Des Prez. Ercole I knew so much music himself that a singer of the Papal chapel in 1481 claimed him as *dell'arte nostra vero monarca* ("the very monarch of *our* art"). A chronicler reports that the duke responded to a serious Venetian military threat by playing the lute and singing for his own solace. It is proper that the boulevard named after him, which the tourist follows on his walk from the central Castello to the Palazzo dei Diamanti, is aesthetically the most satisfactory in Ferrara.

Obrecht died in Ferrara in 1505, the same year as Ercole I, probably of the plague, although he had spent most of his life in his native Netherlands. One may judge the attraction of Ferrara by the fact that his only known trips away from home were to the court of Ercole I. The association began in 1474 when Obrecht, about thirty years old, was among the first foreigners to be hired by Ercole for the newly established court chapel. He did not stay long; but when he had established himself as *famosus musicus* in Bruges, in his position as *succentor und zangmeester* at St. Donatius, he applied for and was granted a special six-month leave in 1487 to visit Duke Ercole in Ferrara. (Another link between Italy and Bruges comes to mind: the Michelangelo "Madonna and Child" which, commissioned by some Flemish merchants, contemporaries of Obrecht, has been worshiped in the Notre Dame Cathedral of Bruges since 1506.) When Obrecht died on his third, and last, trip to Ferrara eighteen years later, the epitaph of a local poet praised him as *Musicus . . . doctus nullique secundus arte vel ingenio* ("an erudite musician second to none in art and genius"). An anecdote, often repeated since the sixteenth century, which credits Obrecht with composing a whole Mass cycle within a single night gives an idea of his superior technical mastery but not of the spiritual beauty that has kept his music alive. His works, the first of the Netherlands Renaissance composers to be collected in a modern scholarly edition, comprise thirty volumes.

The details of Josquin Des Prez's engagement by the Este court prove that bureaucracy and music are old bedfellows.

Ercole I was undecided whether to offer a position to Josquin Des Prez or to Heinrich Isaac, either one a composer of the highest order. A letter from the duke's secretary written around the turn of the century and now preserved in the Archivio di Stato in Modena proposes Isaac because he "is able to get along better with his colleagues and is likely to compose new pieces more quickly. It is true that Josquin is the better composer, but he does it only when it suits him and not when someone else wishes him to ['fa quando li piace, non quando l'homo vole']. And he wants 200 ducats salary whereas Isaac will take 120." Although Ercole, in this instance, could have done no wrong either way, he deserves our increased admiration for not preferring the "organization man" and for hiring the more expensive Josquin (whom history has rightly placed above Isaac).

Ercole was honored directly by a Mass which Josquin wrote, quite literally, on his name. The unifying melody of the Mass, the so-called *cantus firmus,* consists of notes which are derived from the vowels of the title, *Hercules Dux Ferrariae: re ut re ut re fa mi re* (the last diphthong is represented by one vowel only). The corresponding modern names are *d c d c d f e d.* This technique of drawing a melody from an extramusical source is not unique, nor need one overrate the significance apart from the applied wit. A theme *cavato dalle vocali,* extracted from the vowels, or from the profile of the Andes, or from telephone numbers, provides initial material which matters less than what the composer will make of it; and Josquin did well with his employer's name.

He did well in other respects, too. A house apparently went with the high salary, and twenty-seven singers and an organist helped him realize his autonomous musical wishes. The international spirit of the Este family is reflected by some of Josquin's activities. Philip I, the father of the future Emperor Charles V, asked Ercole in December 1501 to lend him

Josquin (*di prestarglielo*) for a trip to Spain. The Duke of Ferrara sent him as a representative of the composer a beautiful *Salve Regina* for five voices as a present. Josquin also traveled to Flanders to hire singers for Ercole (just as a concert manager today would travel to foreign parts for a similar purpose) and opened a bank account in Bruges for this purpose.

The borrowing and lending of musicians seems to have been a favorite activity of Ercole I. When King Charles VIII of France, the only son of Louis XI, spent some time in Lombardy on his fantastic and unsuccessful trip to recapture Constantinople from the Turks, he received from Ferrara "i migliori sonatori di piffero, di flauto e di trombone," i.e., the best band players. Musical traffic was particularly heavy between Ferrara and Mantua, where Ercole's beautiful daughter Isabella, an accomplished lutenist herself, was leading a brilliant life as the wife of Francesco Gonzaga, the fourth Marquis of Mantua. In abundant correspondence one reads of urgent requests for players, singers, composers, instruments, musical advice, or at least a few days leave for a specially needed performer. Later in the sixteenth century, the Este court in Ferrara risked personal and political tension by granting sympathy and ready asylum to the composer Giaches de Wert, who was placed in jeopardy by the Gonzagas in Mantua.

Ercole's wife, Eleanora d'Aragona, was a famous harpist in her own right. No wonder that their son Alfonso I, who succeeded to the dukedom in 1505, remained thoroughly imbued with music. History books usually mention his mechanical skill and his deadly artillery; his impressive portrait by Titian in the Metropolitan Museum of Art in New York shows him leaning against a cannon. His musical interests seem to have given him at least equal pleasure. As a youngster he mingled freely with the employed musicians and reaped considerable embarrassment when one of the singers, Jean de

Gascogne, using the intimacy for unwise political plots, was cruelly punished. Alfonso's wedding in 1501 to the notorious Lucrezia Borgia made musical and histrionic history. The whole cycle of Plautus' comedies was performed, the acts and plays interrupted by dances, concerts, and comic musical entertainment. This mixture of stage, poetry, and music led directly to the creation of opera at the end of the *cinquecento*. Lucrezia Borgia actually balanced the first two wild decades of her life (for which her family was really more responsible than she) by a graceful second half, charming the Ferrara court by her wit and musical interest. A medal coined in her honor shortly after her marriage appropriately shows Amor and a collection of musical instruments on one side, her profile on the other.

Alfonso I had hardly mounted the throne when, in familiar tradition, he tried to secure the musical services of a Fleming, Anton Brumel, who had become famous as a composer and singer at Chartres Cathedral and subsequently as director and instructor of the boys' choir at Notre Dame in Paris. The seriousness of Alfonso I's efforts is reflected in a long correspondence stretching from May to December 1505: to an annual salary of one hundred ducats he added a bonus of another hundred ducats, a house in Ferrara free of charge, and an advance expense account for horses and the journey. Brumel did not accept the tempting offer. Actually Alfonso I was so much out of funds in 1510 that he dissolved his expensive musical establishment, but he took care of his musicians by sending them to his wealthy and sympathetic sister Isabella in Mantua. A few years later, as soon as his finances permitted, he revitalized in full splendor the musical activities in Ferrara. Among the composers he attracted, Bartolomeo Tromboncino and Adrian Willaert emerge as the strongest personalities. When the latter, after leaving Ferrara, soared to illustrious eminence in his long tenure as music director at San Marco in Venice, he always preserved in loyal and grateful memory the graciousness of the Este court. One should like to imagine the conversations he must have held with Ariosto, who was employed in the same household at the same time.

Whatever the glamour of his own wedding to Lucrezia Borgia may have been, Alfonso I tried to surpass it when arranging the wedding of his son and successor Ercole II. The bride was the daughter of the French king; and the year, 1529, the same in which the Turks overran Europe as far as Vienna. The menu has been preserved, as have been the names of all the participating musicians—singers, instrumentalists, a huge crowd altogether. The main feature was the exact correspondence of concert numbers with the dishes served, a kind of planned musical commentary on the gustatory experience; and it is difficult to say which accompanied which. The bridegroom's brother, the Cardinal Ippolito, also gave a concert on the same occasion in the Palazzo Belfiore near the Porta degli Angeli (at the end of the modern Corso Ercole I° d'Este). The palace no longer exists, but the cardinal's style can be easily imagined by anyone who has seen his country house, the Villa d'Este, in Tivoli. His musical initiative may be measured by his entrusting the entire musical preparations for the wedding concert to a twenty-one-year-old, Alfonso della Viola. The bridegroom must have liked the music; for when he ascended to the rule five years later, he made Alfonso della Viola music director at the court. This musician was the first to accompany a dramatic action throughout with music. Although much of the dialogue was sung by alternating four-part choruses, who thus resolved the drama into madrigals, the four performances he produced in Ferrara between 1541 and 1568 claim our interest as forerunners of opera, which sprang up in Florence before the century came to a close.

It has been said that the musical life of a state mirrors the political. The sentence attributed to Confucius and echoed by Plato, that music and government have a common goal and are directly connected with each other, can be confirmed by sensitive ears today. It is illustrated by the life of Ercole II's son, Alfonso II. His rule was long, from 1559 to 1597, and the power of the Este house at its peak. But he died childless, and with him the Este government of Ferrara came to a sudden end. This proximity of ripeness and decay, of fulfillment and annihilation, resounds in the music around him. His love for the art was as genuine as that of his predecessors. He could sing and play himself. He founded an academy where music was carefully cultivated. He showed a touching reverence for his grandfather's court musician Adrian Willaert, who had left Ferrara before Alfonso was born, by paying for the printing of some of his motets and then by visiting the venerable octogenarian at San Marco in Venice. Alfonso's musical establishment became international gossip. Montaigne commented on it in France. Archduke Rudolf of Austria was welcomed on a state visit by about sixty singers and players. "Quando cantano si sente un'armonia che par proprio venghi dal cielo," reports a letter on a similar occasion. ("When they sing, one hears a harmony that seems to come from heaven.") Philippe de Monte, the luminous musician of the Habsburgs, sent Alfonso several madrigals from Prague in the hope that they would be sung by those most gentle spirits and divine voices, "da quei gentilissimi spiriti et divinissime voci." He added his regret that his advanced age would not permit him to visit Ferrara in person "per poter godere tanto bene," where one can have such a good time! Orlando di Lasso, who did visit Ferrara in 1567 and again in 1585, reported his impressions to his employer, the Duke of Bavaria, in such enthusiastic terms that the duke wrote almost jealously to Alfonso II: "Orlando non può più lodare la musica mia." After hearing the music in Ferrara, Orlando no longer could praise the establishment in Munich. Beyond question, almost all the famous musicians of Europe passed through Ferrara under the reign of Alfonso II at one time or another. Even Palestrina, who was indifferent to other offers, including one from the emperor in Vienna, spent four years, from 1567 to 1571, at the Este household in Ferrara, where he must have met Torquato Tasso.

Could all this splendor end suddenly just because the ruler died? The replacement of the Este dynasty by the Holy See doubtless influenced the cultural life of Ferrara. But the musical energy of the city, so eminent for several centuries, could not have vanished overnight if the establishment of the last Este had not contained in itself a treacherous malady which we can uncover in various strange symptoms. Music had changed from a spiritual power to a luxurious entertainment (not unlike what is happening today). In a parallel development, superior craftsmen, sure of their moorings, were superseded by amateurs (i.e., "lovers" rather than "knowers") in confused need of experiments. Universal tradition was abandoned for personal expression. True, this yielding of counterpoint to strumming, of disciplined technique to tentative groping, was typical of the entire period and of most of Europe; but the suddenness of Ferrara's collapse serves as a lesson.

Experiments had begun when Alfonso was a little boy. Nicola Vicentino was the music teacher at the Este court. He had studied with the sage Willaert in Venice, but now the discipline of the old music seemed unsatisfactory to him. He claimed to rediscover the old "enharmonic" and "chromatic" tone systems of the Greeks. He announced his compositions as being of a new order (*composti al nuovo modo*). He invented several instruments on which "new notes" could be played that had not been utilized before. He advocated composing by fancy (*di fantasia*) rather than by discipline. He also publicized his experiments and inventions in pamphlets and polemics. Alfonso's *maestro di cappella,* Luzzasco Luzzaschi, dramatizes the dilemma of an artist floating between tradition and experiment. He was solidly trained, as his activities as organist and composer in the cathedral reveal, but the proximity of Vicentino's newfangled instruments and of the amusement-hungry court tempted him to subordinate musical thought to expressive communication. His madrigals abound in quick alternations of tempos, textures, and unrelated harmonies. Unexpected tones lend color to brief motifs, and melody fragments are abruptly formed.

The effect on the Ferrara court was great. Alfonso's son-in-law, Don Carlo Gesualdo, Prince of Venosa, was so impressed that he began himself to compose in a new vein. Ruthless by nature (he had killed his first wife before marrying Eleanora d'Este), he wrote with an amateur's lack of restraint that actually anticipated many harmonic accomplishments of the late-Romantic era. Where angels fear to tread . . .

Alfonso II himself, though both well-trained and well-intended in musical matters, added to the dilettante atmosphere by volunteering ample criticism at rehearsals, which must have undermined the professional authority of his maestros like Luzzaschi and others. It is reported that he occasionally conducted his own compositions. Increasingly he favored the participation of music-loving (i.e., literally, amateurish) citizens among the instrumentalists and singers at his court; and while this broadening of musical activities may be praiseworthy if one is concerned primarily with "community orchestras" and "community choruses," the loss of music as a spiritual force is a heavy price to pay.

There was even a ladies' orchestra at court. A contemporary cavalier describes how the ladies, carrying various wind and stringed instruments, silently assembled at a long table; when the *maestra del concerto* (probably Tarquinia

Molza who deserved the surname *l'Unica*) entered and with a long polished stick gave the signal to begin, the ladies played with marvelous unanimity. Ladies can, of course, play as well as men; but the emphasis on sex would make it appear that, like lady wrestlers, they were here being used simply for amusement.

The social implications become even more unsavory when one realizes that Alfonso II was the first—and last—Este to engage only Italians as music directors. Cyprian de Rore, who as Willaert's pupil and Luzzaschi's teacher was a significant link in an international tradition, had been the last "foreigner"; but he had been hired by Alfonso's father Ercole II and was promptly dismissed by the new ruler.

At Alfonso II's death in 1597, Ferrara lost the benevolent rule of the Este family and all further claim to musical glory. Monteverdi hardly knew how prophetic he was when, sending his fourth book of madrigals from Mantua to Ferrara in 1603, he opened the printed dedication with an expression of deep regret over Alfonso's death rather than with the expected tribute to the substitute recipient, the Accademia dei Intrepidi.

A few monuments, still visible to the traveler today, bear witness to the disintegration of the former musical vitality. The organs in the Duomo and in the Renaissance church of Santa Maria in Vado (near the Palazzo Schifanoia) may look as handsome as in the days of the Este. Except for the organ in the right choir of the Duomo, however, the original pipes have been replaced (often because the metal was needed for military purposes), the sensitivity of the mechanism has been dulled, and the sound of both instruments has become undistinguished.

Similarly, various opera houses have not fared well. The Teatro Comunale of 1798, across the street from the Castello Estense, has a nondescript past; and one hopes that the current restoration will not merely reinstall the old décor but also imbue the new paint with new life. The Teatro Ristori, behind the Palazzo Comunale, opened in 1622 as an ambitious and praiseworthy civic enterprise. The original wooden structure was subsequently replaced by one of stone. Of the rococo elegance, at best one narrow façade is preserved, whereas the interior has been redone into a vast and modern cinema.

In the Via Frescobaldi No. 40, not far from the center of town, the two-story house in which Girolamo Frescobaldi spent his early years is still inhabited, the tan bricks projecting a nonaristocratic elegance. His father, a well-to-do citizen of Ferrara, had bought it in 1584, one year after Girolamo was born. Alfonso II was still alive, and the young boy imbibed much of the splendor of the Este atmosphere. But when he was twenty, Ferrara could no longer hold him (as it might have a generation earlier). Girolamo Frescobaldi moved to Rome where he became *il più famoso organista dei nostri tempi,* the most famous organist of the Italian Baroque.

New Yorkers, in particular, will appreciate another man's emigration from Ferrara. Giulio Gatti-Casazza, the general manager of the Metropolitan Opera Association from 1908 until 1935, years that included part of the "golden era," began his career as impresario and manager in Ferrara, where he is also buried.

FLORENCE

THE PALACE OF the Bardi family occupies a uniquely prominent place in the history of music but not in the guidebooks. The traveler will find it at Via de' Benci No. 5, halfway between the Uffizi and the church of Santa Croce. A plaque honors a Bardi owner of the late Renaissance for his *valor militare* before spelling out the somewhat biased claim that he returned the art of music, barbarized by the foreign Flemings, to the sublimity of Greek melopoeia. Antiques are now sold in the courtyard, and private apartments fill the vast number of rooms. The mansion incites considerable reflection, for here opera was born at the end of the sixteenth century.

An art form usually is not "born" in a place and at a time easily designated; but opera was as consciously and deliberately created by a group of men around Count Giovanni de' Bardi as a crystal is created in a chemical laboratory. He belonged to the oldest Florentine aristocracy, i.e., to a family of wool merchants who had become rich bankers and, during the Hundred Years' War, moneylenders to the sovereigns of both France and England. Cosimo de' Medici, in the fifteenth century, had married a Bardi girl, and one may hope that he was bolstered as much by her love as by her social position. Giovanni de' Bardi was an intelligent man of many interests. In 1580 he published a treatise on football playing in Florence, and about the same time (he was in his midforties by then) he also wrote a *Discourse on Ancient Music and Good Sing-*

ing. The latter had grown out of regular discussions held in his home by a group of scholars and artists, who became eventually known as the *camerata Fiorentina.* Among them were the composers Jacopo Peri and Giulio Caccini (surnamed Romano), the poet Ottavio Rinuccini, the musical scholar Vincenzo Galilei (the astronomer's father), and the aristocratic amateur musicians Pietro Strozzi and Jacopo Corsi.

The main concern of the *camerata* was the revival of classic Greek music—an obvious endeavor when seen as a parallel to the Renaissance revival of Greek sculpture and architecture. On the assumption (which was correct) that Greek tragedies were originally sung rather than merely spoken, the Florentines reached the conclusion (which was faulty) that music should always be subservient to words rather than remain autonomous. The implications were intelligently discussed in letters and tracts, and experimentally demonstrated in new works. As a result, a modern musical style was developed, the *stile rappresentativo,* in which communication and expression flourished at the expense of musical structure and complexity.

Giovanni de' Bardi discoursed in the following fashion: "In composing, you will make it your chief aim to arrange the verse well and to declaim the words as intelligently as you can, not letting yourself be led astray by the counterpoint like a bad swimmer who lets himself be carried out of his course by the current and comes to shore beyond the mark that he has set, for you will consider it self-evident that, just as the soul is nobler than the body, so the words are nobler than the counterpoint. Would it not seem ridiculous if, walking in the public square, you saw a servant followed by his master and commanding him, or a boy who wanted to instruct his father or his tutor?"

Because rational words rule supreme, absolute music is an error which Galilei wants to correct: "If the object of the modern practical musicians is, as they say, to delight the sense of hearing with the variety of the consonances, and if this property of tickling (for it cannot with truth be called a delight in any other sense) resides in a simple piece of hollow wood over which are stretched four, six, or more strings of the gut of a dumb beast or of some other material, disposed according to the nature of the harmonic numbers, or in a given number of natural reeds or of artificial ones made of wood, metal, or some other material, divided by proportioned and suitable measures, with a little air blowing inside them while they are touched or struck by the clumsy and untutored hand of some base idiot or other, then let this object of delighting with the variety of their harmonies be abandoned to these instruments, for being without sense, movement, intellect, speech, discourse, reason, or soul, they are capable of nothing else. But let men, who have been endowed by nature with all these noble and excellent parts, endeavor to use them not merely to delight, but as imitators of the good ancients, to improve at the same time, for they have the capacity to do this and in doing otherwise they are acting contrary to nature, which is the handmaiden of God." Galilei's remedy is the sacrifice of all contrapuntal accomplishments to a simple vocal line: "La parte più nobile importante e principale della musica . . . sono i concetti dell'animo espressi col mezzo delle parole, e non gli accordi delle parti come dicono e credono i moderni pratici" ("The noblest, most important, and principal part of music are the concepts of the soul expressed by means of words, and not the sounding together of several voices as the modern practitioners say and believe").

According to the conviction of the *camerata,* music had steadily declined "since the Greeks lost the art of music along with their worldly power." But now in Florence, "let us at least endeavor to give poor unfortunate Music a little light,"

Count Bardi admonished his club members. The response to his encouragement was the production of a work that, having very little resemblance to Greek tragedy, yet has become immortal as the first opera in history—not the only instance where the enthusiasm of dilettantes has released unexpected consequences.

Pietro de' Bardi, Giovanni's son, witnessed these early ventures as a youngster and described them in a letter forty years later:

"Giulio Caccini, considered a rare singer and a man of taste, although very young, was at this time in my father's *camerata,* and feeling himself inclined toward this new music, he began, entirely under my father's instructions, to sing ariettas, sonnets, and other poems suitable for reading aloud, to a single instrument and in a manner that astonished his hearers.

"Also in Florence at this time was Jacopo Peri, who . . . received high praise as a player of the organ and the keyboard instruments and as a composer of counterpoint and was rightly regarded as second to none of the singers in that city. This man, in competition with Giulio, brought the enterprise of the *stile rappresentativo* to light, and avoiding a certain roughness and excessive antiquity which had been felt in the compositions of Galilei, he sweetened this style, together with Giulio, and made it capable of moving the passions in a rare manner, as in the course of time was done by them both.

"By so doing, these men acquired the title of first singers and inventors of this manner of composing and singing. Peri had more science, and having found a way of imitating familiar speech by using few sounds and by meticulous exactness in other respects, he won great fame. Giulio's inventions had more elegance.

"The first poem to be sung on the stage in *stile rappresentativo* was the story of *Dafne,* by Signor Ottavio Rinuccini, set to music by Peri in few numbers and short scenes and recited and sung privately in a small room of the Palazzo Corsi. I was left speechless with amazement. It was sung to the accompaniment of a consort of instruments, an arrangement followed thereafter in the other comedies. Caccini and Peri were under great obligation to Signor Ottavio, but under still greater to Signor Jacopo Corsi, who, becoming ardent and discontent with all but the superlative in this art, directed these composers with excellent ideas and marvelous doctrines, as befitted so noble an enterprise. These directions were carried out by Peri and Caccini in all their compositions of this sort and were combined by them in various manners.

"After the *Dafne,* many stories were represented by Signor Ottavio himself, who, as good poet and good musician in one, was received with great applause, as was the affable Corsi, who supported the enterprise with a lavish hand. The most famous of these stories were the *Euridice* and the *Arianna;* besides these, many shorter ones were set to music by Caccini and Peri. Nor was there any want of men to imitate them, and in Florence, the first home of this sort of music, and in other cities of Italy, especially in Rome, these gave and are still giving a marvelous account of themselves on the dramatic stage. Among the foremost of these it seems fitting to place Monteverdi."

The *Euridice* is the earliest opera of which the music—by Peri and Caccini—has been preserved. The first performance took place on the evening of 6 October 1600 in the Palazzo Pitti. The visitor wandering through the gallery today will tax his imagination guessing at the exact room. The occasion, in any case, was the festivity for the wedding of King Henry IV of France and Maria de' Medici. Whoever remembers her as the ambitious regent after her husband's murder in 1610, initiating intrigues and fostering revolts against her own son Louis XIII and the powerful Cardinal Richelieu, should not forget her role as guest of honor at the *Euridice* premiere. We must assume that she did not like opera, for there was no transfer of this new art form to France until after her death half a century later.

Dafne came a few years earlier, probably in the carnival of 1597, but the music is lost. Giovanni de' Bardi spent the years around the turn of the century away from Florence: he had accepted a position as chamberlain (*maestro di camera*) and officer in the private guard of Pope Clement VIII. The *camerata* had to move its quarters from his palace on the Via de' Benci No. 5 to that of the noble Jacopo Corsi on the Via Tornabuoni No. 16–20. Today the Corsi palace accommodates the Banca Commerciale Italiana. Around 1600 it was known as a "headquarters of the Muses" (*un continuo albergo delle Muse*) and a hospitable meeting place for artists and scholars (*quasi una pubblica accademia a tutti coloro che dell'arti liberali avessero intelligenza o vaghezza*). It was in this Palazzo Corsi that *Dafne* was first heard in the presence of *Don Giovanni Medici e d'alcuni de principali gentiluomini de la città.* Jacopo Corsi apparently not only financed the venture but also played the harpsichord at the premiere, and there were several repeat performances in his house in the course of the next years. The American opera fan today can find a copy of the original *Dafne* libretto in the Library of Congress in Washington; and he can find the patrician Rinuccini house, where it was written, on the Via de' Rustici No. 2 (behind the Palazzo Vecchio) in Florence. He may wish to put a flower on the simple tombstone of Jacopo Peri in the church of Santa Maria Novella, between the fourth and fifth pillars on the left aisle. In any case, he owes it to himself to make a pilgrimage to the Bardi and Corsi palaces where opera as an art form was originally created and first heard.

Before leaving the *camerata,* we must relate a moralistic detail. Vincenzo Galilei had been properly concerned with reviving the ethical implications along with the expressive qualities of Greek music. His *Dialogue on Old and Modern Music* leads a technical discussion up to the following conclusion: "It is impossible to find a man who is truly a musician and is vicious . . . The man who has in his boyhood used every necessary means and proper care to learn the science of the true music, devoting to it all his labor and effort, will praise and embrace everything that accords with dignity and honesty and will denounce and flee from the contrary, and he will be the last to commit any ugly or unseemly action, and gathering from music most copious fruits, he will be of infinite advantage and utility both to himself and to his state, nor will he ever, in any place or at any time, do or say any inconsiderate thing, but will continually be guided by decorum, modesty, and reverence."

Be that as it may, Galilei's colleague in the *camerata,* Giulio Caccini, with Peri the composer of the first operas in history, broke the confidence shown to him by a member of the Medici court; and his act of denunciation led to the murder of Eleonora of Toledo by her husband Piero de' Medici, the brother of the ruling Grand Duke Ferdinand I. Caccini's bad personal reputation in Florence must have been drowned out by the trills and vocalizations he taught to a whole generation that was growing up with the new music. *Le donne di Giulio Romano,* a small vocal ensemble formed exclusively by his two successive wives and his daughters, became so popular that Maria de' Medici, Queen of France, invited the group to Paris for a few months; and Grand Duke Ferdinand I did not permit Caccini and his ladies to extend their tour to England lest Queen Elizabeth lure them away from Florence forever.

It is an ironic fact that today there is little opera heard in Florence (except for the annual commercial May festival which is presented, in the main, neither by nor for Florentines). The opera lover in Florence can find considerable consolation—visual and fanciful, it is true, rather than aural—in a visit to the Teatro della Pergola. It stands on the Via della Pergola No. 12–32, east of the Duomo, on the way from the Museo dell'Opera del Duomo toward the Convent of Santa Maria Maddalena dei Pazzi and the English cemetery (depending on whether one wants to see a celebrated Perugino fresco or Elizabeth Barrett Browning's tomb). The superintendent lives in the building at No. 20 and is likely to offer a conducted tour for a friendly request and a nominal gratuity. The Teatro della Pergola, notwithstanding several alterations, has preserved the original construction of 1656. The architect was Ferdinando Tacca, the son of Pietro Tacca whose two odd Baroque fountains moisten the Piazza Santissima Annunziata. Commissioned by a private club, the Accademia degli Immobili, he transformed a warehouse of the wool workers on a Florentine back street into one of the most beautiful and elegant opera houses in the world. What the visitor will see need not be described; what he wishes to imagine must be mentioned.

The Teatro della Pergola, for at least two centuries after its inauguration, represented the musical life of Florence. Opera successes of other towns and countries quickly found their way to the Via della Pergola, but the record of first performances is impressive. The list of composers who enjoyed a *prima assoluta* there includes Paisiello, Salieri, Gluck, Donizetti, Verdi, and Mascagni. Cherubini's father Bartolomeo was *maestro al cymbalo* of the Teatro della Pergola in the latter part of the eighteenth century—on the conducting staff, one would say today. No wonder that Luigi, the tenth of twelve children, had several of his early operas performed in the house before abandoning Florence, where he was born, for Paris, where he became famous. (Another native Florentine opera composer became a hero in Paris; but Lully was a fourteen-year-old *garçon de la chambre,* and the Teatro della Pergola not yet built, when he emigrated: the musical life of Florence owes him nothing.) It was at the Teatro della Pergola, also, that the major operas of Meyerbeer and of Mozart were first performed in Italy. *Robert le Diable, Les Huguenots, Le Prophète,* and *Dinorah* all reached Florence within a decade of their respective premieres in Paris, and considerably before being heard in other Italian towns. Mozart's *Figaro* traveled intact from Vienna to Florence in two years; and *Don Giovanni* made it from Prague in five. Considering that Italy outside Florence waited for these two Mozart operas until 1811, one reacts with special feelings to the fact that Mozart's *Die Entführung aus dem Serail* was first performed in Italy also in the Teatro della Pergola in 1935, 153 years after it was written.

The traveler, more aware of the Duomo than of either the Bardi and Corsi palaces or the Teatro della Pergola, might rightly wonder whether the secular entertainment of opera deserves to represent the musical life of Florence. A historian of the city, Ferdinand Schevill, has explained the worldly orientation of Florence: "Arising not as an ecclesiastical but as a trading center, the town directed its awakening intellectual curiosity to the immediately pressing problems of public and private conduct. In other words, it turned to the Here and away from the Hereafter, which was the chosen land of the scholastic doctors. By this shift of attention a movement of worldliness or secularization took its place by the side of the prescriptive contemplation of the Heavenly City and gradually overshadowed it."

This shift of attention can be seen by anyone standing before the Fra Filippo Lippi "Madonna" in the Palazzo Medici, for instance, and realizing that the blonde girl depicted was the painting friar's mistress. The same point can be illustrated by the musician who, from a plethora of parallel events, will choose three examples as characteristic for the worldly utilization of a religious framework: a holiday, a church musician, and a book.

The octagonal baptistery is the central building, and St. John the patron saint, of Florence. Already in the thirteenth century, his midsummer holiday was celebrated with gay music. The chronicler Villani, a contemporary of Dante, reports that St. John was feasted with games, entertainments, and balls for the whole population. Men and women walked through the city "with trumpets and various musical instruments," frolicking gaily through the streets during the day and reassembling for more music and pleasure at the noon and evening meals. This custom lasted for centuries. Brunelleschi, the creator of the cupola of the Duomo, built a float for one of these holidays; and a connection can be made between these early impromptu combinations of spectacle and music with the later development of opera. In form, the Florentines made little difference between honoring St. John and reveling during the carnival. No other city has produced an equal number of carnival songs, attractive tunes to mixed texts, which amuse the musician today in his home as much as they did the crowd along the Arno half a millennium ago. Even the distinguished Lorenzo il Magnifico and Heinrich Isaac contributed to this literature.

In the fourteenth century, the church organist Francesco Landini was the most celebrated musician in Florence, and perhaps in all of Italy. He was still young when Villani devoted a long paragraph to him in his *Book on Famous Citizens of Florence.* Landini lost his eyesight as a child after an attack of smallpox, but "he began to play the organ with such art and sweetness that he surpassed all other organists without comparison . . . Consequently, by common consentiment of all musicians, who conceded to him the palm of this art, he was publicly crowned with the laurel in Venice by the illustrious king of Cyprus, as the Caesars used to do to poets." His compatriots recognized that he was *cieco del corpo, ma dell'anima illuminato,* "physically blind but spiritually illuminated." The Secretary of the Republic recommended him to the Bishop of Florence with the words: "A glorious reputation for our city and a light for the Florentine church comes forth from this blind man." Landini's tombstone of 1397 in the church of San Lorenzo (in the wall of the second chapel in the right aisle) shows him, obviously blind, holding a portable organ; and two angels above him complete the trio with viol and lute. The point to be made is that the legacy of this worthy church organist is entirely secular: of his 154 preserved compositions, all, without exception, are worldly songs, mostly madrigals and ballads. This "turn to the Here and away from the Hereafter" is amply corroborated by Landini's role in a Renaissance story, the *Paradiso degli Alberti* by Giovanni del Prato. The country house of Messer Alberti in the Florentine hills is a paradise in which a group of men and women meets to indulge in food, wine, love, music, dance, storytelling, and conversation. Francesco Landini is prominent among the guests. He plays and sings *moltissime ermonie,* "very many compositions"; he recites a novella; he asks, in high spirits, for his portative organ, and his love songs are so tender that everybody's heart bursts with joy; he applauds two ballad-singing girls; and finally he initiates a discussion on musical differentiation among birds by observing that a sparrow and a nightingale have reacted differently to his organ playing.

The book, our third example, can be brought into the actual presence of the modern traveler, unlike Landini's paradise. The Biblioteca Laurenziana, accessible from the cloister of San Lorenzo, was designed and begun by Michelangelo to house, among other treasures, the private library of the Medici. The Codex Squarcialupi (Med. Pal. 87) is exhibited under glass on desk No. 20 on the left, about the middle of the hall.

Other manuscripts in the Biblioteca will rightly appeal to the visitor's curiosity and attention; but the Codex Squarcialupi occupies a unique position among musical sources. Singularly magnificent in execution and exceptional in being folio size, it is one of a handful of sources transmitting to us the music of the fourteenth century in Italy (with Boccaccio and Petrarch among the poets represented). If Florence executed "the prescriptive contemplation of the Heavenly City" with lute accompaniment, as it were, the Codex Squarcialupi mirrors this attitude by being entirely secular, although commissioned by the organist of the Duomo and copied by a friar. In this respect it is typical rather than special; for of the total of over five hundred *trecento* compositions that have been preserved from an area with Florence at its center, only ten relate to church service. The continuity of this secular orientation is emphasized by the lapse of at least a century between the composing and the collecting of these songs.

The person of Antonio Squarcialupi, whose name on the flyleaf has been appropriated by the codex, provides a welcome lead to an inquiry into the musical contribution of the Duomo, which cannot be entirely ignored. Squarcialupi's feats on the organ coincided with the consecration and completion of the Duomo and with the Renaissance magnificence of Cosimo, Piero, and Lorenzo de' Medici. Musicians from England and Scandinavia crossed the ocean to hear him play at Santa Maria del Fiore. The King of Hungary, Matthias Corvinus, sent him a special envoy to study the construction of pipe organs. Lorenzo Il Magnifico entrusted to him the musical education of his children, among them the later Pope Leo X; insisted on his company when traveling to the thermal springs of Morba to relieve his gout; and wrote (like Marsilio Ficino, Angelo Poliziano, and others) an epitaph on his death in 1480 which is quoted below Squarcialupi's bust, attributed to his contemporary Benedetto da Maiano, in the left aisle of the

Duomo just before the gigantic equestrian paintings by Andrea del Castagno and Paolo Uccello.

Brunelleschi's beautiful cupola, the completion of which prompted Cosimo to proceed with the consecration of the cathedral of Santa Maria del Fiore, seems more concrete than the music heard on that occasion. Yet Dufay's Mass *Nuper Rosarum Flores* is equally real to the senses; it is representative of the period; and it is immensely gratifying to the person who is guided by his ears no less than by his eyes. One can hear Dufay's Mass today, but can only imagine the spectacle staged by Cosimo. He had chosen the 25th of March 1436, which was the Feast of Annunciation in the church calendar and the first day of the New Year according to the very private tradition of Florence. Pope Eugene IV, who was living at the time in the Dominican monastery of Santa Maria Novella, walked all the way to the Duomo on a raised and carpeted boardwalk, tiara-crowned and in white, attended by seven cardinals in red and thirty-seven bishops and archbishops in purple, followed by the resplendent array of the city fathers, and greeted by festive banners and garlands of fresh flowers. The music for the Mass that was celebrated represented actually a gift to Florence; for Guillaume Dufay belonged to the Papal Chapel, and the title (and hence musical substance) chosen for the Mass implied a clearly understood compliment to the Lady and the City of the Flowers. The election of the Pope five years earlier had been celebrated by a grand motet, *Ecclesiae Militantis,* of Dufay's, and so had the peace conference of Viterbo between the Pope and the emperor in 1433.

If Dufay was still singing as well as conducting in these performances, he was rewarded shortly after the Florence consecration by a canonry in Cambrai, where he spent most of the remainder of his long life. There need be no doubt about his superior position in all music history. As one of the creators of the Netherlands school, he has been compared, by analogy, to Jan van Eyck; and the traveler familiar with the quality of the painter can estimate that of the musician. Before the end of the fifteenth century, the compiler of the earliest dictionary of musical terms, Joannes Tinctoris, could write in Naples that before Dufay "recently deceased . . . there does not exist a single piece of music . . . that is regarded by the learned as worth hearing."

The Florentines on that March day in 1436 recognized the value of what they were hearing, and they did not forget it. Thirty-one years later, on 1 May 1467, Squarcialupi addressed his northern colleague in the following words: "My venerable Father, rightly to be honored above all others! With the greatest joy to my soul, I have read and often reread your most humane letter; and I embraced with all my heart the fellow-singers whom you sent, the best of your church, just as you wrote, and having heard them, I am easily induced to believe it. They are, indeed, absolutely excellent, both in sweetness of voice and in the knowledge and the art of singing, and worthy of you, their teacher. It is not possible to tell you how much this has pleased our Magnificent Piero de' Medici, who loves you very much, dear father, and always speaks of you with great respect. And he asserts what I can freely agree to, that you are the greatest ornament of our age. Also Lorenzo de' Medici, the son of Piero, regards you with admiration. Because of the excellence of his divine talent, [Lorenzo] enjoys quality in all the arts, and thus he delights exceedingly in the greater refinement of your music. And for that reason he admires your art and respects you as a father. . . ."

Dufay had all along maintained direct contact with the Medici family. His letter to Cosimo's sons Piero and Giovanni, written one year after the fall of Constantinople, may be quoted in full: "Magnificent and Noble Sirs, All Humble Commendation Beforehand! Since I well know that you have always taken pleasure in song and since, I believe, you have not changed your preferences, I have felt encouraged to send you some chansons which, at the request of some gentlemen of the King's court, I composed recently when I was in France with Monseigneur de Savoye. I also have some others which I shall send you at another time. In addition, in this past year I wrote four Lamentations for Constantinople which are rather good: three of them are for four voices and the texts were sent to me from Naples. I do not know whether you have them there. If you do not have them, be so kind as to let me know and I shall send them to you. Furthermore, I am very much pleased with Francesco Sacchetti, your representative here, for during the past year I was in need of something at the court of Rome and he helped me most magnanimously and treated me most graciously for which I extend my unceasing thanks. I understand that you now have some good people in your chapel at San Giovanni and because of this, if it pleases you, I should like to send you some of my little things more often than I have done in the past. I do this also out of my regard for Antonio [Squarcialupi], your good friend and mine, to whom I beg you commend me cordially. Magnificent and noble sirs, if there is something which I can do here for your lordships, please let me know and I shall do it with all my heart through the aid of our Lord, who I hope will grant you a good and long life, and at the end paradise. Written at Geneva, the 22nd of February. Your humble chaplain and unworthy servant, Guillaume Dufay, Canon of Cambrai."

For the fact that there were "some good people in the chapel of San Giovanni," i.e., in the baptistery, most of the credit must go to the Medici family. Cosimo, in particular, had put the organization of the chorus on a practical, sound basis by keeping the church singers in his private employ as well. After the completion of the Duomo, the same chorus also provided the music in the big building. One must not imagine a large choir. The gay *cantoria* friezes by Luca della Robbia and Donatello are now in the Museo dell'Opera del Duomo; but in the fifteenth century the crowd of dancing, playing, and singing children adorned the two little balconies, left and right of the central dome, on which the chapel singers assembled. If the traveler today gasps for breath on his climb, he does not have to sing after reaching the choir balconies through a little door in either sacristy. The space on each balcony can hardly accommodate more than fifteen performers across (a second row would be possible only by standards of a New York subway crowd). The actual number fluctuated from five to about a dozen, and the resonance of the big building was an expected and needed ally.

The Medici, from Cosimo through Lorenzo, tried their utmost to create a good chorus. An ambassador to the Holy See is advised "that he seek as best he can to engage a *magister capelle* and three singers or more, as is deemed necessary for the chapel, and that he may have the authority to spend up to two hundred florins yearly for the said singers." The branch manager of the Medici bank at Bruges reports to Piero that he could not persuade an excellent tenor in Antwerp to move to Florence, but that he had hired another singer for whom he would assume the financial responsibility in case Piero should not like his voice. On the whole, however, the chorus in the Duomo never flourished really well, and the turnover of singers was rapid. The Estes in Ferrara and the Sforzas in Milan apparently proved more attractive to the best singers, notwithstanding such lures in the contracts offered to the Florentine singers as "the laundering of all their clothes . . . the barber who will shave them once a week . . . a new beret for the feast of St. John . . . ten lengths of good cloth for a jacket for Christmas."

The chapel choir occasionally went on tour: in 1458, for instance, the "singers of Florence" celebrated the Easter

Mass in Modena, and the Feast of the Assumption in Siena. When, inversely, the singers of the King of Naples visited Florence (for the same kind of political reasons that today lead to a cultural exchange program), the account books list not only "extraordinary expenses . . . for having Antonio's [Squarcialupi's] small organ brought to the church [of the Santissima Annunziata] and carried back again" but also "food expenses, 15 soldi for 35 eggplants, and 54 soldi for 6 flasks of Trebbiano at 9 soldi the flask, and ten soldi for thirty white breads, and ten soldi for fruit, all of which were bought in order to entertain the singers of the King of Aragon."

The one great musician in Florence in the period before the fall of the Medici was Heinrich Isaac, Squarcialupi's pupil and successor at the organs in the baptistery and the Duomo. Of Flemish origin, he became a Florentine by choice. He married a Florentine butcher's daughter, lived in the city for twenty years before Lorenzo's death and Savonarola's temporary success drove him to the court of the Emperor Maximilian I in Innsbruck and Vienna, and returned to Florence in his old age. Lorenzo's son Giovanni had been his pupil; and now, as Pope Leo X, he took care of the composer's last years "perchè il poveretto viene vecchio," and because he remembered Isaac as "cantore et compositore singularissimo alias servitore carissimo della buona memoria di Lorenzo de' Medici."

Lorenzo Il Magnifico had treated him like a personal friend. They made chamber music together, for Lorenzo could hold his own in musical matters. At his house, Isaac mingled with Poliziano, Botticelli, and Ghirlandaio—their equal in spirit, knowledge, and grace. Isaac's affection for his patron is touchingly audible in the lament on Lorenzo's death, composed on Poliziano's poem, *Quis dabit pacem populo timenti?* ("Who will now give peace to the fearful people?").

It was not Savonarola's severity toward church music ("artful music is rather injurious in church than useful . . . it does nothing but charm the ear and the senses") but the merchant and banker's traditional desire for entertainment that gave the music of Florence a secular tinge even in a religious setting. We have encountered many examples, but this attitude is nowhere more poignantly illustrated than in an experience of the most spiritual Florentine of all times. Dante meets in purgatory his old friend Casella, a composer whom he knew in Florence (and of whom, by the way, no music has been preserved). They assure each other of their affection beyond the grave ("così com'io t'amai nel mortal corpo, così t'amo sciolta"), and then Dante asks Casella for some music. He remembers how the composer's songs used to calm all his wants, and he now needs solace for his soul which is distressed by the anguish of the journey. Casella obliges, not with a sacred composition, but with a love song; and when Dante says that the sweetness of the *canzone* made all who heard it so content that they cared about nothing else, even in purgatory, he has defined the role of music like a true citizen of Florence.

LUCCA

LUCCA BOASTS OF five successive generations of composers named Puccini—a record surpassed only by the seven generations of Bach north of the Alps. Lucca also leans on a long tradition of theatricals with music. The connection of a Puccini with the theater is much older than the *Turandot* fan might suspect.

Viewing the obvious traces of the Roman amphitheater in the marketplace, the Piazza del Mercato, and learning of the documented evidence of a coetaneous theater, one must try to remember that the old Romans liked shows as much as do modern New Yorkers, and that the productions contained not only lions and gladiators but also musicians. The local Christians inherited the appetite for games and tried to reconcile public entertainment with religious devotion by cultivating several original customs, all of them accompanied with music.

The San Martino Cathedral preserves a wooden crucifix of Oriental origin in the small octagonal marble temple in the left aisle. The Sacred Countenance, or *Volto Santo,* has attracted pilgrimages from all parts of Europe for many centuries. The legend of the minstrel offering in naïve piety music and dance as a supreme gift to God has been claimed by divers cities. Massenet's opera places the jongleur in Notre Dame in Paris. The legend seems to be at home in Lucca; its particular character suits that of the city, and a woodcut by Burgkmair attests to the widespread association of the story with the *Volto Santo.*

The special holidays, on 13 and 14 September, are celebrated in a fashion worthy of the legendary minstrel. Heinrich Heine's 1829 description (in the second volume of his *Reisebilder*) fills in the details in a vivid and personal manner. The crucifix is carried across the city in a colorful procession. Its return to the cathedral is marked by a High Mass and a concert piece especially composed for the occasion. In Lucca this special composition was known as the *mottetone;* but though on a grandiose scale, it was not so much a motet as a concerto for soloists, two choruses, two orchestras, two organs—all in all, well over two hundred participants. Flourishing since the seventeenth century, the *mottetone* composed in honor of the Sacred Countenance adopted so many qualities reminiscent of the musical jongleur that the Vatican, in Pope Pius X's edict on music, *Motu Proprio,* of 1903, specifically banned the continuation of the practice on the grounds of its profane and operatic character. All four of Giacomo Puccini's ancestors contributed to the *mottetone* literature, and the last and most famous composer of the line found at least a comparable outlet in the first-act finale of *Tosca.*

An interdict from a different side put to an end another form of musical entertainment unique to Lucca. The local government, independent since the Middle Ages, was elected by a public vote every three—later every two and one half—years. The ballots were slipped into pocketlike receptacles; and the *festa delle tasche,* the Feast of the Pockets, celebrated each new government with a musical show that lasted three days. Whether a *tasca* may properly be called an opera is a moot question: there is no doubt about the unrestrained participation of music in an elaborate and often allegoric stage representation. The composers and poets had to be citizens of Lucca. The native Puccinis among themselves composed thirty-two *tasche* in the eighteenth century alone. This gay custom, which dated back to 1431, was terminated by Napoleon in 1799, together with the freedom of the republic.

Giacomo Puccini's ancestors were respectable musicians and elegant citizens. All of them were organists and choirmasters at the Duomo San Martino. The idea of a hereditary claim was so strongly imbedded in the minds of the Lucca authorities that the future composer of *Madama Butterfly* was legally designated to the post when he was five years old. His father Michele had just died, and the immediate successor had to agree to the clause that he "should and must hand over the post of organist and *maestro di cappella* to Signor Giacomo, son of the aforementioned defunct master, as soon as the said Signor Giacomo be able to discharge such duties."

All of the early Puccinis, each in his turn, studied music in Bologna after the founder of the musical line, the first Giacomo, had documented his preference in an extensive correspondence with Padre Martini. This worthy Franciscan (whom the reader of this book remembers from Bologna) also taught Giacomo's son Antonio and was probably instrumental in the latter's admission to the famed Accademia Filarmonica in 1771, one year after the same honor had been bestowed on Mozart. Giacomo and Antonio were also directors of the Cappella Palatina, a vocal and orchestral organization maintained by the city since 1490 until its dissolution in 1805 in the wake of Lucca's political surrender to Napoleon. Contrary to the contemporary American idiom, the singers of the Cappella were identified as musicians (*musici*) and the players as instrumentalists (*violinisti*). The wide reputation and the actual accomplishment of the Lucca orchestra emerge nicely from a letter by the fourteen-year-old Mozart to his sister: "I have heard and seen the great festival of St. Petronius in Bologna. It was beautiful but very long. They had to fetch trumpeters from Lucca for the salvo, but they played abominably."

The dignity and fame of the early Puccinis must not be minimized. The first Giacomo made it clear to the city fathers that the cathedral organist, although on the same municipal payroll, deserved a higher salary than the public executioner; and his claim for a distinct status was recognized by the token payment of an extra loaf of bread each month. Giacomo's voluminous diaries, now preserved in the State Archives of Lucca, illuminate many facets of the musical life from 1748 to 1777. Both he and his son Antonio were listed in several music dictionaries, including the illustrious *Biographie Universelle des Musiciens* by the Belgian Fétis. Domenico Puccini, the third in line, matched his father's accomplishment when he, too, was admitted to the exclusive Bologna Academy; and almost half a century after his time, he was joined with Bach, Handel, and Beethoven in an album published by Breitkopf und Härtel in Leipzig. Except for the founder of the musical dynasty, all the other Puccinis wrote operas; and thus *Le Villi* may be considered not just the beginning of an individual career but also the continuation of similar efforts across four generations.

The last and best-known of all Puccinis was born in 1858 in a house at Via di Poggio No. 30, which was marked by a tablet exactly one month after his death in 1924. It is a narrow street that opens quickly and directly into the dazzling façade of the church of San Michele. The family lived in the spacious rooms on the second floor (*primo piano*). Giacomo Puccini showed his affectionate sentimentality for the place by buying it back with the help of *Manon Lescaut* after his mother's death in 1884 had forced the family to sell it. Lucca offered good musical training to the boy, as one might expect of a community of which the history names a music teacher in the sixth century and records a continuous practice of music education—first in the cathedral school and later in other churches and private quarters—since the eighth century. Giacomo's father Michele had been a director of the conservatory and inspector of Lucca's school music. The Istituto Musicale Luigi Boccherini (as it was renamed in 1943 in honor of the two hundredth birthday of another renowned native musician) had been organized shortly before Giacomo's birth. It stands near the eastern Porta Elisa where the sounds of the practicing students and of the bustling citizens do not interfere with each other. Now his uncle, Fortunato Magi, was in charge before moving on to the more glamorous position as director of the Liceo Benedetto Marcello in Venice. Magi taught his nephew personally; and the composer of *Turandot* related his nervous habit of jerking his leg in response to bad singing to the pedagogic kicks on the shin received from his uncle for wrong notes. Before leaving Lucca at twenty-two for study in Milan, Puccini played the organ at the cathedral and other churches. According to his own story, he secretly sold organ pipes for cigarette money, carefully avoiding the missing tones in his harmonizations, but he enriched his Sunday improvisations by the addition of folk songs and opera tunes. Of his church music written in those early years, an *Agnus Dei* has found its way into the second-act madrigal in *Manon Lescaut;* and the rest need be neither mentioned nor heard.

Bernard Shaw called Puccini "the heir of Verdi." We can apply the connection, if we wish, to an external detail of their respective lives. Just as Verdi returned as a landowner to his native countryside around Busseto after studying in Milan and reaping early successes, so Puccini built himself a villa in his native province. Torre del Lago (which has been officially renamed Torre del Lago Puccini) is a dull, dusty, and flat village less than twenty miles outside Lucca, but it permitted Puccini to indulge in his favorite sport of hunting wildfowl. He considered it his home from 1891 until 1921, when the opening of a peat factory near his villa, with the concomitant attack on several of his senses, drove him four miles up the coast to Viareggio (just in time to help raise money for the centennial of Shelley's drowning and cremation in the presence of Byron). His Viareggio house, which has imparted his name to the piazza on which it stands, is neither noteworthy nor accessible. His villa in Torre del Lago is open to the public and reveals to the visitor divers deposits of the composer's personality. Here he worked near an upright Förster piano on all his operas from *La Bohème* to *Turandot,* often in the presence of people in his study, provided they ignored him, and mostly with a hat on his head while writing the score. He is buried in the wall behind the piano in a small mausoleum built by his son.

In addition to the Puccinis, who remained, Lucca produced a host of good musicians who left. In the sixteenth and seventeenth centuries, Lucca musicians set the tone not only in Venice and Genoa but in Munich, Baden, and Antwerp. In the eighteenth century, Luigi Boccherini became an international success. He was born in an attractively located house on the Via Fillungo No. 71 but moved to Rome as a student when he was only fourteen years old. His prowess on the violoncello is reflected by his invention of the string quintet with his own instrument doubled and favored. Vienna, Paris, and Berlin feted him; and Madrid became his last home. One hundred and twenty-two years after his death in Spain, his remains were returned in 1927 to the church of San Francesco in Lucca. His tomb, in the left wall between the second and third altars, shows his profile in bas-relief. Next to it, a plaque honors the memory of Francesco Geminiani, a Lucchese who spent most of his life in England and Ireland. There he had some contact with Handel but independently gained fame and success for his mastery of the violin as a performer, composer, and teacher. His Italian temperament may partly explain his reputation in England for two seemingly excessive passions: a *tempo rubato* and a picture collection.

Another native of Lucca who did not stay in town was Alfredo Catalani, four years older than Giacomo Puccini and his rival in the esteem of Verdi and Toscanini. Of his four operas, *La Wally* (after whom Toscanini named his older daughter) reached distant European countries and both Americas.

Fastened to the ground, however, is a beautiful theater. The Teatro Comunale del Giglio of 1692 was remodeled by the Bourbons in the early nineteenth century without being the worse for it. Entering through the stage door on the right flank (at No. 15), the visitor might find satisfaction even in the summer silence of the auditorium.

MANTUA

THE RICH MUSICAL past of this town hardly reaches the ears of the casual visitor of today if he listens exclusively to the guides and guidebooks. At best he will be told spurious stories about Rigoletto, the court jester whose activities in Mantua have been placed on the operatic stages of all the world by Giuseppe Verdi. Postcards can be bought showing the house, wall, and garden from which Gilda was abducted; and an official sign marks the original on the Piazza Sordello No. 23, on the same square as the Palazzo Ducale. Any friendly bus driver on the road to Verona will be quick to point out an inn with a square tower, on the left roadside at the end of the causeway, as Sparafucile's hideout where the Duke of Mantua declared that "La donna è mobile." Actually all references to Rigoletto in Mantua are postcard fairy stories; for it is well known that the locale of Piave's libretto (founded on Victor Hugo's *Le Roi s'amuse*) was originally the French court, and Rigoletto the court jester of King Francis. The Austrian censors, apprehensive after the 1848 unrest of any slur on any monarch's character, forced Verdi and Piave to transplant the scene from France to Mantua even though the libretto and much of the music had been completed.

To the real and substantial glory of Mantua's musical past, the modern traveler is led by a modest hand-lettered sign to the left of the entrance to the Sala degli Specchi in the Ducal Palace. It has survived primarily because it is painted directly on the wall, and it reads: " 'Ogni Venere Di Sera Si Fa Musica Nella Sala Degli Specchi' Cl. Monteverdi al Card. Ferdin. Gonzaga Da Mantova Il 22 Giugno 1611." (" 'Every Friday evening there is music in the Mirrors Gallery' Claudio Monteverdi to Cardinal Ferdinand Gonzaga of Mantua, 22 June 1611.") This sign is to the imagination of the musician what the Mantegna frescoes, in the same palace, are to the eye. Claudio Monteverdi is one of the giants of music history. His collected works, in a modern edition, comprise sixteen volumes. He was born in 1567 in nearby Cremona as the eldest son of a well-to-do doctor and was employed from 1590 until 1612 as musician at the court of Vincenzo I Gonzaga, Duke of Mantua. Starting as a *suonatore di vivuola,* an orchestra fiddler, he was promoted four years later to *cantore* and finally in 1601 to *maestro della musica del Ser. mo. Sig. Duca di Mantova,* director of all musical activities, secular and religious, at the court. He spent the last thirty years of his life, 1613–43, in Venice, where we think of him in St. Mark's Cathedral.

In Mantua, Monteverdi not only performed as one of the seven string players at the court but also composed for all occasions. He married the daughter of one of his colleagues who used to sing at various court concerts. The duke, according to the customs of the times, hardly ever traveled without his musicians. Monteverdi accompanied him to Austria and Czechoslovakia on a campaign against the threatening Turks, and to the Netherlands on a pleasure and health trip. The influence of these journeys, together with Monteverdi's superior musical imagination and craft, soon produced works that quickly placed him in the forefront of the "modernists." He was the target of a famous pamphlet by Artusi, among others, entitled *The Imperfection of Modern Music.* His answers were both literary and musical. His statement ". . . e credete che il moderno compositore fabbrica sopra li fondamenti della verità" (". . . and believe me that the modern composer builds on the fundaments of truth") became the battle cry of the "modern" practice. His opera *La Favola d'Orfeo,* which was performed in Mantua in 1607, definitively established the success of the new style.

What was considered modern in Monteverdi's time? The break in musical style around 1600 was as decisive as it is today. The conservatives were writing complex and masterly motets, full of contrapuntal subtleties, which followed scholarly laws and which, moreover, obscured the words. The moderns insisted that the text must always be understood, for their main concern lay with expression. The music was simplified accordingly—often reduced to mere accompanying chords (as, for instance today, in a guitar accompaniment to a song) and relegated to the role of handmaiden to poetry and expression. One immediate result of the new trend was the creation of opera, artificially concocted by a group of well-meaning dilettantes in Florence in the 1590's. Suffice it to say that it was Monteverdi in Mantua, with his rare sense for music as well as drama, who removed opera once for all from the experimental and anemic atmosphere in which it was born.

The success of *Orfeo* was so great (it is still being performed) that Monteverdi followed it up by two more music dramas, *L'Arianna* and *Ballo dell'Ingrate,* on the occasion of the elaborate wedding celebrations for Francesco Gonzaga and Margarita of Savoy in 1608. A chronicler of the festivities reports: "After the cardinals, princes, and ambassadors were seated, the customary trumpet signal was given from the center part of the stage. After the trumpets had sounded for the third time, the great curtain suddenly opened. One saw clouds that were constructed so artistically as to seem real. Beneath them, waves were visible, surging back and forth, and from them there gradually emerged the head of a woman. It was Manto—she who once founded Mantua. In slow measured movements she arose and by this time the trumpets had ceased their playing. She reached a small island and, standing there in the rushes, she sang to the accompaniment of instruments set up behind the scene, with such sweetness that all her listeners were carried away." All these operas were performed in the Ducal Palace, in the Sala degli Specchi, perhaps also in the Sala dei Fiumi, and certainly in the Teatro della Corte (the latter now in bad repair, used as a warehouse, and closed to the public). One sometimes wonders how this new art form "opera" would have survived its childhood diseases without the healthy treatment given to it by Monteverdi.

It is worth remembering that Monteverdi's employer Vincenzo Gonzaga was also the protector of Tasso and Rubens. Although we have no testimony to a meeting between Rubens and Monteverdi (it is unlikely that two such masters working in the same household for about eight years should have ignored each other), we do know that Rubens' salary of four hundred ducats yearly was about twice that of Monteverdi, who was his elder.

Among the musicians sharing the Gonzaga court with Monteverdi was Salomone Rossi, a Jew, and so respected for his contribution to chamber music in the new style (as well as to the Jewish synagogue service in Mantua) that he was permitted to move around the city without the yellow mark that all Jews were required by law to display on their headgear.

At the same time, the organist at the Duomo was Lodovico Grossi da Viadana. He was among the first to abstract a continuous bass line from the complexity of a polyphonic score; and this "comfortable invention for every sort of singers, and for the organists," as he called it on the titles of several works, became a characteristic of the whole musical Baroque. Viadana's practice of using a *basso continuo* helped establish the supremacy of harmonic thinking; and the contraposition of bass and melody has remained a live principle to this day in musical instruction and composition.

On his tour through the palace, the visitor is likely to be shown the Gabinetti Isabelliani, the special apartments built, about one century before Monteverdi, for Isabella d'Este by her husband Francesco Gonzaga. Isabella, the sister-in-law of Lucrezia Borgia and also of Lodovico Sforza il Moro, was the prototype of a Renaissance princess, an extraordinary woman in every way. The drawing of her face by Leonardo da Vinci (often reproduced after the original in the Louvre) remains unforgettable, with its strong profile among soft contours. Her interest in music was genuine. Her proficiency on the lute was acclaimed in verse. To the names of Leonardo, Titian, Mantegna, Ariosto, and Castiglione, which are readily associated with her, there must be added, of equal stature, those of the Netherlands musical masters Johannes Ockeghem and Josquin Des Prez. The latter, closely allied to the Este family in Ferrara, visited her personally. The former reached her from France by his music. One of his compositions, the canonic chanson *Prenez sur moi,* decorates in beautiful intarsia the wall of the music room in Isabella's apartment. Whereas the composition, one of the most popular and frequently printed of Ockeghem's, can be easily transcribed and performed, nobody has quite figured out the meaning of the many musical rests above the door. Are they just decorative? Or a private joke? Or a suggestion not to produce any uncalled-for sounds?

One can easily guess that the rich musical activities around Isabella in 1500 and around Monteverdi in 1600 are not islands but part of a long stream of musical tradition in Mantua. Dante has celebrated the birthplace of Virgil and of the troubadour Sordello. During his lifetime, the "city band" of Mantua, the *pifferi e trombetti,* was so famous all over Italy that it was invited to Naples and Milan as a *cosa nuova.*

Throughout the Renaissance, Mantua attracted players, singers, organists, composers, organ builders, and music theorists from the whole of Europe. Gafori, Josquin Des Prez, Agricola, Compère, Tromboncino, Cavazzoni, Viadana, and Frescobaldi are just some of the names. Palestrina rejected an invitation to the court (shortly before Monteverdi accepted one) by insisting on an inordinately high salary to compensate for his lucrative fur and leather business in Rome.

One other musical monument will attract and reward the tourist in Mantua, although it is presently not even listed in most guidebooks. A private club, the Accademia Virgiliana, founded in 1767, maintained an orchestra of eighteen players and engaged the architect Antonio Galli-Bibiena, who had gained fame in the preceding decade by his new opera house in Bologna, the Teatro Comunale, to build a special theater for the activities of the academy. The Teatro Scientifico was opened in 1769. The following year, on 16 January, the fourteen-year-old Mozart gave a concert there during his first journey to Italy. The event is commemorated by a plaque in the building, which is otherwise in bad repair. The entrance is from the Via dell'Accademia No. 47, near the Piazza Dante Alighieri, and a tip to the janitor will ensure admission. Even in ruins, the auditorium presents an exciting sight of late-Baroque theater architecture. There are plans afoot (1962) to restore the theater and make it accessible to practical use.

The Mozarts enjoyed themselves in Mantua. The father thought that in all his life he had never seen a more beautiful theater. The boy looked "as if he had been through a campaign," for the winter air and the open fires had tinged his face reddish-brown, particularly around the nose and mouth. The concert was a big success. The crowd, which was traditionally admitted free of charge because of an imperial subsidy to the academy, shouted, clapped, and cried "bravo." The program, occasioned by the arrival of the *espertissimo giovanetto,* the most expert youth, Signor Amadeo Mozart, is worth reproducing if only to convey an idea of the musical appetite of the Mantuans:

1. Symphony composed by Signor Amadeo.
2. Harpsichord concerto shown to him and executed by him at sight.
3. Aria by a professor.
4. Harpsichord sonata played at sight by the young man with appropriate variations of his invention, and later repeated in a key different from that in which it is written.
5. Violin concerto by a professor.
6. Aria composed and sung at once by Signor Amadeo, improvised, with proper accompaniments executed on the harpsichord, on a text expressly prepared for, but not first seen by, him.
7. Another harpsichord sonata, composed and played simultaneously by the same, on a musical motive proposed to him impromptu by the first violinist.
8. Aria by a professor.
9. Oboe concerto by a professor.
10. Musical fugue, composed and executed by Signor Amadeo on the harpsichord, and brought to the proper conclusion according to the laws of counterpoint, on a simple theme presented to him at sight.
11. A symphony by the same, concertized with all parts on the harpsichord, on a violin solo placed before him impromptu.
12. Duet by professors.
13. Trio in which Signor Amadeo will improvise the violin part.
14. The latest symphony composed by the afore-mentioned.

After the concert the Mozarts went back to the Hotel Croce Verde (to which the first house with portico on the Corso Umberto I°, No. 24–30, now corresponds).

MILAN

THE SPIRIT OF Leonardo da Vinci still dominates the city and promises to outlast the new glass skyscrapers which appear to overpower it temporarily. Leonardo's statue graces the central Piazza della Scala, the square in front of the opera house. His "Last Supper" holds a spell over millions of people who have made a pilgrimage to the old Dominican convent in the western quarter of the city. The Pinacoteca Ambrosiana, the picture gallery in the somber palace, a short walk from the Duomo, built by Cardinal Federigo Borromeo in 1609, contains priceless treasures in many rooms, among which none radiates a greater fascination than the Sala del Leonardo. Here one can view his drawings and notebooks. Of two paintings ascribed to him, one represents a musician and catches our attention for various reasons. It portrays an exquisitely handsome young man whose long golden locks are topped by a brilliant red beret. When the portrait was cleaned in 1905, a music manuscript appeared in the lower right corner, held in the young man's right hand. The composition was identified as having been written by Franchino Gafori; and as the features did not deny known representations of Gafori on various woodcuts found in his books, Leonardo's portrait opens new vistas on the personality of this superior Renaissance musician. Gafori directed the music in the Duomo (and thus much of the musical life of Milan) from 1484 until his death in 1522. He was generally revered as the most erudite musical scholar of his time. His undiminished reputation caused Leopold Mozart three hundred years later to list him, in the short chapter on history in his *Treatise on Violin Playing,* among a handful of musical writers who "have earned great credit in the scientific world."

Leonardo's friendship alone could vouch for Gafori's extraordinary qualities, which were not restricted to, nor necessarily in conflict with, his blond curls, beautiful face, and sensitive fingers. Leonardo was not the man to waste his time on inferior intellects and superficial artists. He knew much music himself; wrote about it in his notebooks and in *Paragone;* and proved his firsthand relation to music by singing in tune, playing the lute and the viol, and experimenting with the shape and construction of several musical instruments. His life-span (1452–1519) coincided almost exactly with that of Gafori (1451–1522). Leonardo lived in Milan from 1483 to 1499. When Gafori moved to Milan in 1484, they were both in their early thirties. Their friendship developed quickly, for experts seem to agree that the portrait was painted around 1485. As a sidenote one might mention that on Napoleon's orders the painting was kept in Paris from 1796 until 1815 and that after returning to the Pinacoteca Ambrosiana it was identified in the catalogue as a portrait of Lodovico Sforza (whose swarthy grossness one knows well from other pictures).

Gafori's life and work are representative of the musical history of Milan in the Renaissance and hence well worth relating. He was born in Lodi, some twenty miles outside Milan. (There must be something in the air of Lodi: Mozart wrote his first string quartet there, just passing through the town.) His father was a *condottiere,* a professional military leader of mercenary soldiers (like Gattamelata, immortalized in Padua by Donatello, or like Colleoni in Venice by Verrocchio). His mother sent him to a nearby Benedictine monastery where he learned Latin and music without, however, becoming a monk. The traveler passing through Lodi on the way from Milan to Mantua or Bologna might pause to think that the Lodi Duomo was three hundred years old when the boy Gafori sang in the choir, and that the neighboring church of the Incoronata was built and richly decorated while Gafori was active in Milan. A brilliant and attractive young man today might spend his third decade, the beginning of his mature professional career, along lines similar to those followed by Gafori in the fifteenth century. He gave private music lessons, wrote and published a few essays, composed occasional madrigals and motets, and moved around through a number of short-termed jobs. He joined his father at the Gonzaga court in Mantua. He caught the attention of the Doge Adorno, who called him to Genoa. In Naples he searched out the company of Tinctoris, who had just printed the first musical dictionary. In Bergamo he is said to have modernized the organ in Santa Maria Maggiore by the revolutionary introduction of a pedal. By that time, at the age of thirty-two, he had established himself so well that he was offered the signal position of music director at the Duomo in Milan. As is true today, some positions paid in prestige rather than in cash: moving from Bergamo to Milan, Gafori actually accepted a reduction in salary from one hundred lire imperiali annually to ninety-six. One is right in assuming, however, that a metropolis like Milan soon provided sources of extra income, although his official salary at the Duomo was never raised during the remaining thirty-eight years of his employment and life.

Gafori's duties as music director in the Duomo were clearly defined. He sang in the choir (in which Josquin Des Prez had sung some years earlier, from 1459 to 1472), directed the choir, and trained the voices of the choirboys. He was much interested in reforms and must have enjoyed being a successful administrator. He introduced special robes for the singers, appointed a "notator" to take attendance at rehearsals, in-

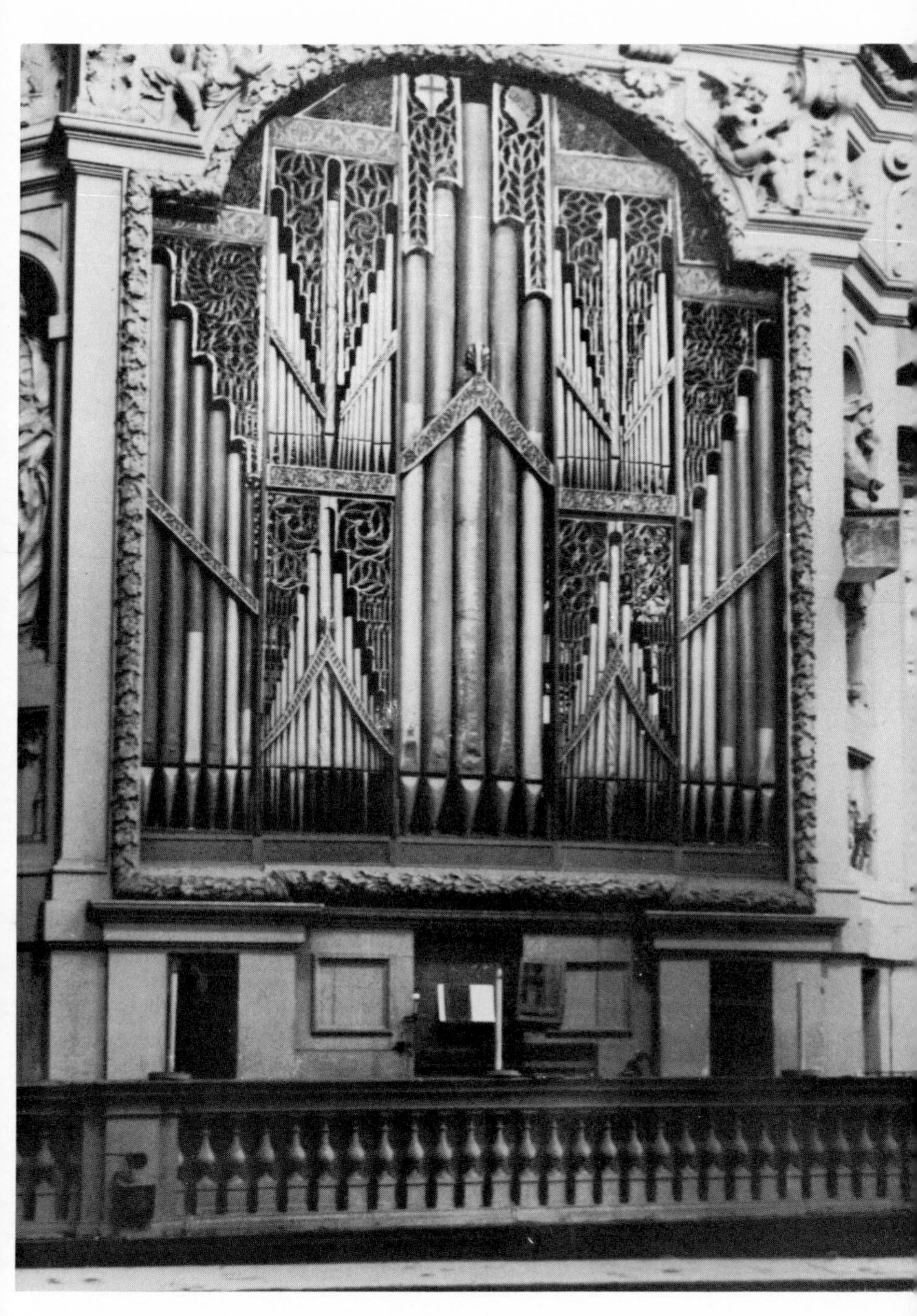

BOLOGNA: The organ of 1470 in San Petronio.

BRESCIA: The Antegnati organ in San Giuseppe.

BRESCIA: The Teatro Grande.

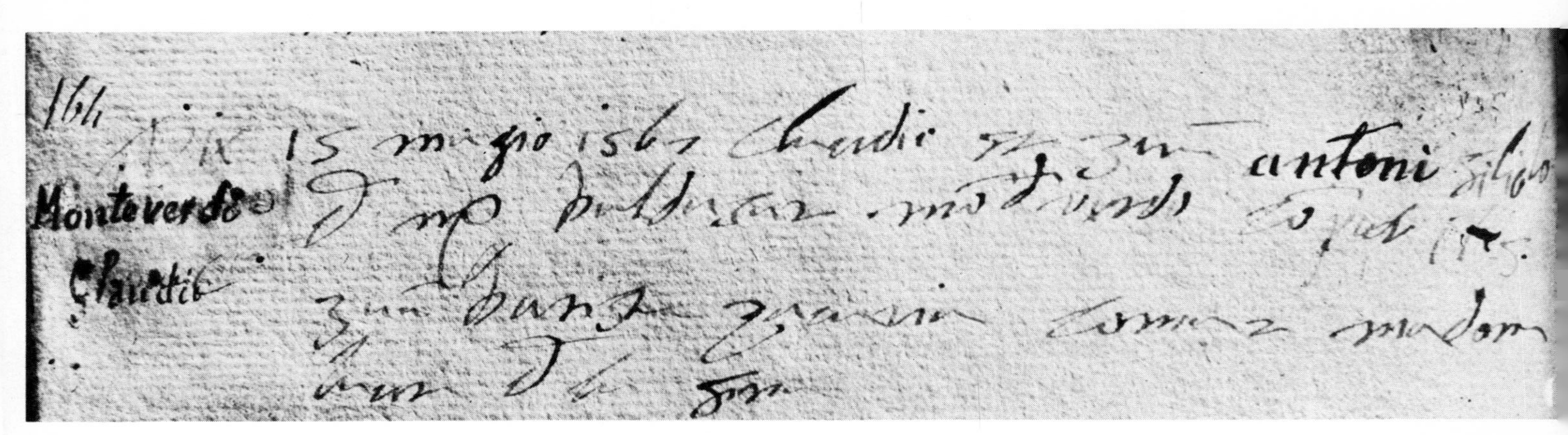

CREMONA: The record of Monteverdi's baptism in the church of Sant'Abbondio.

FLORENCE: The Bardi Palace where the *camerata* met.

FLORENCE: The Corsi Palace where the first opera was performed.

FLORENCE: Landini's tombstone in San Lorenzo.

LUCCA (Torre del Lago Puccini): Puccini at his piano.

MANTUA: The Sala degli Specchi in the Gonzaga Palace where Monteverdi made music every Friday evening.

ORVIETO: Angels by Signorelli with string and brass instruments.

PALESTRINA: The house in which Giovanni Pierluigi was born.

PARMA: Merulo's tomb in the Duomo.

RAVELLO: Klingsor's enchanted tower.

ROME: Villa Medici.

ROVERETO: The Corso Bettini with the Teatro Zandonai on the right beyond the cypress trees, and the former Albergo della Rosa at the end of the street.

VENICE: Bella's painting of a concert in an Ospedale.

sisted on cash fines for unexcused absences, and fired singers for lack of discipline. He also prevailed in his effort to double the size of the adult chorus from five to ten and to engage an expensive and famous tenor. At the same time he improved the quality and the behavior of the boys' choir by reducing the size from thirty to about fifteen and by preferring boys from socially well-to-do families. As a reward and incentive for the best boys, he secured some scholarships. Financial statements that have been preserved in the Duomo archives often refer to his *prudentiam ac solicitudinem,* his prudence and careful concern.

The musical taste of the period was clearly determined by the Netherlands schools, of which the members were widely and thickly distributed all over Europe. The musicians at the Sforza court in Milan, under the leadership of Gaspar van Weerbecke, attracted the most famous Netherlands singers and composers, among them Compère, Agricola, and even the great Josquin Des Prez after he had left the Duomo. Gafori, on his part, hired for the Duomo exclusively Italian musicians —a strange and then rare restriction which may convey a chauvinistic flavor. But there was much healthy contact between the two leading musical organizations of the city. Gafori composed not only motets and Masses for his sacred service but also secular entertainment for Lodovico Sforza, and in return performed appropriate religious compositions of the Netherlands court composers at the Duomo. At some festivities the two forces joined, and the spectacle was enhanced by machines and special music instruments designed and built by Gafori's good friend Leonardo da Vinci.

The music of Gafori combines Italian clarity and suavity of sound with Netherlands polyphonic discipline, but his theoretic treatises elevate him to a special position of musical excellence. Let it be said that, too technical for a discussion in this context, they bring into harmony traditional knowledge and modern speculation. Lodovico Sforza il Moro appointed him *musicae professor* at his newly established school; and when the French occupied Milan, they not only left Gafori intact in his various positions but honored him with the title *Regius Musicus.* He accumulated a distinguished private library in his house near San Marcellino (in the general area of today's central Via Broletto), which was often used for research by Leonardo da Vinci. He presented many of his books to the new church of the Incoronata in his birthplace, Lodi, where they can be consulted today.

As we look at Gafori's portrait in the Pinacoteca Ambrosiana, we should be aware not only of his golden curls and glamorous appearance but of the exquisite Renaissance spirit he incorporates. He reconciled good looks with a good mind, musical performance with theory, voice lessons with university lectures, the Church with the court, scholarly Latin treatises with Italian epigrams and tracts, and an erudite library and religious routine with warm personal friendships and worldly well-being.

The construction of the Duomo was begun almost exactly one century before Gafori, but the musical history of the Duomo begins before the construction. A musical liturgy for the Duomo was defined by a special church council in 1311. Pipe-and-drum corps circulated among the citizens soliciting financial contributions to the edifice. Some of these processions turned into theatrical presentations at which money was collected for the construction. Occasionally a stage was erected on what is now the Piazza del Duomo and *oblazioni e trionfi* were performed—musical shows at which the hat was passed to help cover the cost of the new cathedral. Even in the half-completed church, vocal and instrumental concerts were arranged to appeal to the generosity of the congregation.

Church music in Milan had a long tradition to draw on before the Duomo was finished at the close of the fourteenth century and the music in the Duomo became internationally famous under Gafori's leadership at the close of the fifteenth century. The Roman Emperor Constantine had no sooner proclaimed, in Milan in 313, his edict in favor of the Christians than the city quickly developed into a musical center. The name of Ambrose has left its imprint on both Milan and music. The son of an old Roman patrician family, Ambrose found himself in Milan in 374 as consular prefect of the region when the bishopric became vacant. Seven days after his conversion to Christianity, Ambrose was acclaimed Bishop of Milan. His lasting effectiveness as an administrator, recognized by political and theological experts alike, can be guessed by the traveler who encounters his name not only in the basilica, which Santo Ambrogio founded and where he is buried, in the library, and in the museum, but also in the appellations of hotels, restaurants, dry goods, and sport teams.

His contribution to music is first attested to by a much-quoted report in the *Confessions* of his disciple St. Augustine who delighted in the new Milanese church celebration in which "the brethren were singing together both with voice and hearts" (ix. 7). Ambrose, it seems, used music as a weapon against the military power of the emperor. The latter's family favored the Arian heresy and wanted to seize the Milan basilica for the new sect. When Bishop Ambrose refused to surrender to the heresy, the imperial forces laid siege to the basilica in which Ambrose had locked himself with his congregation. "The devout people watched day and night in the church, ready to die with their Bishop . . . Lest the people should wax faint through the tediousness of sorrow," Ambrose kept them awake by introducing a musical game, as it were, actually an old Oriental custom. The singers were divided in two groups and sang hymns and psalms antiphonally, i.e., by responding to each other now in alternation, now by a repeated refrain. "And from that day to this the custom is retained and still imitated by divers, yea, almost by all Thy congregations throughout other parts of the world."

This heroic episode has left its mark on the typical Milan liturgy as well as on antiphonal singing throughout the Christian Church. But St. Ambrose's contribution to music went further. Realizing, like Luther more than a thousand years later, that an unsophisticated congregation can be wooed and won by community singing, he wrote a number of hymns, and edited others, in which a religious thought is popularized by simple language and an attractive tune. Hymns in general became known as "Ambrosiani" and have entered the realm of folk music.

The sacred chant of the Roman Catholic Church, as we know it today, was written down in a definitive reform under Pope Gregory I around the year 600; and the term "Gregorian chant" has become identical with it. The musical reforms of St. Ambrose preceded those of St. Gregory by more than two hundred years. One is safe in assuming that Milan, more than any other diocese, resisted the Gregorian innovations out of regard for her own Ambrosian heritage. The strict subordination of musical elements under the prayer text, as prescribed by Gregory, is unpopular in a society with a strong musical tradition and orientation.

Is this one of the reasons for the quick emergence of Milan as a stronghold of opera? What real Italian opera does not consider the libretto a mere vehicle for the flow of melody? In any case, the musical center of Milan today is not the Duomo but the Teatro alla Scala. The battle between religious and secular concerns and the irresistible trend in Milan toward the latter are amusing to recall. The true character of a city cannot be repressed, one is ready to assume, by either time or politics.

The musical shows before the Duomo are not the only examples of a skillful adaptation of worldly entertainment for religious purposes. The Spanish rulers of Milan during the Counter Reformation frowned on frivolous songs, but the sensuous Milanese sang madrigals with impunity by lending them pseudo-religious texts. These so-called "contrafacts" of secular madrigals were extremely popular within earshot of the powerful Cardinal Carlo Borromeo. Monteverdi's madrigal books, sought after in nearby Mantua and Venice, were distributed in Milan in a religious adaptation by one Aquilo Coppini. Strict censorship delayed Milan's participation in public operatic ventures, but the courtiers compensated for this deprivation by an excessive cultivation of dance music.

When the rigid Spanish rule of Milan was replaced in 1708 by the pleasure-loving Austrian, the operatic enthusiasm of the Milanese, noticeable but timid in the seventeenth century, broke into the open and has remained unrestrained ever since. By the end of the eighteenth century, the society ladies of Milan had founded an order whose members were honoring the male soprano Luigi Marchesi by wearing a waistband embroidered with his initials. When the prima donna Gabrielli left Milan ("we shall do homage to her as a queen and praise her to the skies," Leopold Mozart writes to his wife from Italy in 1770), 150 carriages of state accompanied her in a glorious farewell procession. Johann Christian Bach, the Leipzig cantor's youngest son, abandoned both his father's style and religion by joining the household of the Milanese Count Litta; as a reward for arranging private musical entertainment for the count, he was appointed organist at the Duomo. Giovanni Battista Sammartini, Gluck's teacher, conducted open-air concerts on the esplanade of the Castello Sforzesco (the park behind it) and in the public gardens by the Porta Orientale (today the Porta Venezia), with an orchestra of sixty in which father and son Boccherini occupied, respectively, the first bass-viol and violoncello chairs.

The two Mozarts, father and son, arrived in Milan at

noon on 23 January 1770, attracted by the lively musical atmosphere of the city and the chance of a major opera commission for the fourteen-year-old Wolfgang. They stayed until the middle of March at the Augustinian monastery of San Marco, which the traveler today may want to inspect just behind the Palazzo di Brera, a ten-minute walk from the center of town.

Leopold Mozart wrote to his wife: "We have three large guest rooms. In the first we have a fire, take our meals and give audiences; in the second I sleep and we have put our trunk there; in the third room Wolfgang sleeps and there we keep our other small luggage. We each sleep on four good mattresses, and every night the bed is warmed, so that Wolfgang, when he goes to bed, is always quite happy. We have a brother, Frater Alfonso, especially for our service and we are very well looked after." The comfortable guest rooms, like the whole monastery, were turned into army barracks by Napoleon's soldiers twenty-six years after harboring the Mozarts. Today they provide quarters for the priest of the adjoining Lombard-Gothic church of San Marco. They have been considerably remodeled and cut up, and the house is altogether in bad repair. The visitor climbing up one flight of stairs in the building to the left of the church will have to discover for himself any imprint made by the Mozarts. There is little doubt that Wolfgang played on the Antegnati organ in San Marco, learning a great deal, like Gluck before him, from the composer and church organist Giovanni Battista Sammartini. (In the same church, Verdi conducted the first performance of his *Requiem* on 22 May 1874.)

Wolfgang wrote to his sister: "Perhaps you think that I have not been having a good time. Indeed, I have, and I cannot remember how often, but I think we have been to the opera six or seven times and then to the festa di ballo which, as in Vienna, begins after the opera, but with this difference that there the dancing is more orderly." The Mozarts were also drawn into the carnival and they "listened to the Requiem Mass for old Marchese Litta, who to the annoyance of his enormous family died during the carnival, although they would have gladly allowed him to go on living until Lent." The important event was a contract for Wolfgang to write an opera for the next Christmas season. After traveling through Italy from March to October 1770, he returned with his father to Milan in time, not only for rehearsing *Mitridate, Rè di Ponto,* but for composing most of it. "I cannot write much, for my fingers are aching from composing so many recitatives. Mamma, I beg you to pray for me that my opera may go well and that we may be happy together again." They went to a Milan tailor because the boy had grown since leaving Salzburg; and the *maestrino* conducted the premiere on 26 December "in a scarlet suit, trimmed with gold braid and lined with sky-blue satin." The opera lasted "six good hours" and was "a success, God be praised, for every evening the theater is full, much to the astonishment of everyone, for several people say that since they have been in Milan they have never seen such crowds at a first opera."

The visible monument to that period is the Teatro alla Scala which, with the blessings of the Empress Maria Theresia of Austria, Duchess of Milan, was opened on 3 August 1778 (while Washington was trying to get the British out of New York and George Rogers Clark was chasing Indians in Illinois). The name "Scala," tempted as one may be to connect it with the many staircases and steps of the tall building, let alone with a musical term, derives from a family. Regina della Scala, married to a member of the eminent Visconti family, had given money and her family name for the construction of a church, Santa Maria della Scala, which four centuries later was torn down to provide the site for the new opera house. The architect, Giuseppe Piermarini, had just redesigned the Palazzo Reale (the royal palace to the right of the Duomo as one faces it), and he knew that he was building in a similar style and color the most modern and spacious opera house then in existence. Actually, the front of the opera house looks today as it did then except for the later addition of the asymmetrical left wing now sheltering the Museo Teatrale. Whether it is a handsome building, the traveler must decide for himself. But there is agreement that the acoustics are good and that the performances have made operatic history by an imaginative selection of new works and consistent adherence to high artistic standards.

The opening was a phenomenal success, with an orchestra of seventy in the pit and an excellent ensemble including thirty-six horses on the stage. The composer was not named on the placards, although he was the famous Salieri, Mozart's Italian rival. His *Europa Riconosciuta* (a good motto for the American tourist in Italy) had been chosen after the great Gluck had declined the invitation to compose an inaugural work. The dignity and decorum of the Teatro alla Scala have been dramatized by several widely circulated and authenticated anecdotes of more recent years. Joining the Scala as a young conductor in 1898, Toscanini battled the audience by not repeating the *Lohengrin* prelude and, worse still, not leaving any time between the two scenes of the third act for chat and drinks. He refused to continue the dress rehearsal of *La Bohème* because Caruso was not singing with full voice. At the close of the 1903 season, the applause of a frantic audience did not let Toscanini continue a performance of *Un Ballo in Maschera* unless the tenor Zenatello were granted an encore in the second scene, The conductor threw his baton at the crowd and walked out in the middle of the performance not to return to the Teatro alla Scala until three years later.

The ukase against encores on the printed programs today is actually almost as old as the building itself. The archives are full of police regulations, dating back to the eighteenth century, which bar encores, signs of disapproval, applause "in a manner which does not represent the true worth of the performance," dogs in the boxes, weapons in the cloakrooms, and masks in the gaming rooms. Gambling, by the way, was forbidden in the city of Milan except in the Teatro alla Scala, where the income from the gaming tables helped finance the operas—a situation duplicated today by the State of New York, where bingo is outlawed except when played in or for churches and synagogues. The local government of Milan remained true to its tradition when it financed the reopening of the Scala after the First World War by special taxes on movies, theaters, football, stadiums, and other more frivolous entertainments.

Measured by the results over the years, the money was well spent. Between 1812 and 1817, Rossini, then in his early twenties, wrote four new operas for La Scala (his total operatic output for the same period was seventeen!). The French commandant of Milan was so pleased with Rossini's *La Pietra del Paragone,* which ran for fifty-three performances in its first season at La Scala, that he exempted him from the military draft—a decision, Rossini commented, worth a whole division to Napoleon. A decade later, Bellini's fame became firmly rooted by a series of premieres at La Scala, climaxed by *Norma* on the opening night of the 1831–32 season. Donizetti was much in evidence in the thirties, but the name of Verdi dominates the remainder of the century. His first four operas, among them *Nabucco,* were all first heard at La Scala, and so were his last two, *Otello* and *Falstaff* half a century later. At the premiere of *Otello* in 1887, the twenty-year-old Toscanini was playing the violoncello in the orchestra. The evening may serve to symbolize the continuity of tradition and quality in the Teatro alla Scala; for just as Verdi's unique eminence among opera composers has become an undisputed historic fact, so has the unmatched glamour of the Toscanini administration at La Scala from 1921 to 1929.

The museum of the Teatro alla Scala in the nineteenth-century left wing provides as satisfactory an experience as is possible in an opera house without music. It even offers a glimpse of the auditorium through a box near the first exhibition room. The visitor's operatic imagination is greatly stimulated by a wealth of autographs, portraits, programs, and mementos among which the prominent Italian figures are joined by Garrick, Rachel, and Asiatic masks. Two rooms, the most personal and intimate of all, are dedicated to Verdi. Upstairs a Liszt piano is incongruously surrounded by prints and drawings of theaters and stage sets of the last three centuries, with Giuseppe Galli-Bibiena himself handsomely represented by his own sketches as well as by a portrait.

Verdi liked to stay at the Grand Hotel et de Milan, No. 29 on the expensive Via Alessandro Manzoni, which leads away from La Scala on the right. The traffic below stopped on the January day in 1901 when he died in one of the rooms. He is buried in the rest home for aged musicians on the Piazza Michelangelo Buonarroti, in the western quarter of Milan, a comfortable and dignified building that he constructed and endowed toward the end of his life. His statue in the square is less of a monument to him than is the well-being of the one hundred musicians inside the Casa di Reposo. He is buried next to his second wife Giuseppina in a little chapel in the back of the courtyard. A tablet commemorates his first wife and her two children, who died early. A reported two hundred thousand people lined the streets at his funeral. At the Teatro alla Scala, Toscanini conducted a memorial concert in which Tamagno, the first Otello, and Caruso, representing the new generation, both participated.

The overpowering position of the Teatro alla Scala should not deter the musical traveler from looking at the Teatro dal

Verme to the left of the huge Garibaldi monument that blocks the Via Dante on the way from the Duomo to the Castello Sforzesco. The inside of the appealing building has been completely revamped into a vast and ugly cinema which is also occasionally used for political rallies. The Via Giacomo Puccini, bordering it on the left, reminds one that Puccini's first opera *Le Villi* was first heard here in 1884; and so was Leoncavallo's *Pagliacci* eight years later under Toscanini's baton.

MODENA

THE TRAVELER WHO has been to Ferrara will remember the Este family at the fountainhead of the musical current. When the Estes lost Ferrara to the Papal State in 1598, the tradition of the family was continued by a sideline in Modena; and one notices with satisfaction how the Este stream in a new bed quickly fertilized this formerly provincial town.

The new duke Cesare d'Este, as soon as the capital had been established in Modena, appointed Orazio Vecchi choirmaster and music teacher to his children. The choice of a native composer was tactful but in this case also artistically most satisfactory. In 1598, Orazio Vecchi was forty-eight years old. Born and raised in Modena, he had acquired a wide reputation as a composer of most attractive madrigals, *canzonette,* and sacred music; and also as a poet, singer, ball-player, and witty conversationalist. Moreover, he was an ordained priest, like many of his compositions facetious and serious at the same time. He had been choirmaster at the Modena Cathedral in earlier years, but poor pay had obliged him to appeal to local charity and eventually to leave Modena for Correggio. There he became an archdeacon and lived in his own house. But the elevation to a capital of his native town in the last decade of the century prompted him to return to Modena; and his work at the new Este court added income and prestige to his improved position at the cathedral. Music must be heard rather than described; yet *Le Veglie di Siena,* encountered in that town, give an approximate idea of Vecchi's intent to use music for expressive entertainment without sacrificing solid craftsmanship. His *Amphiparnaso* of 1594 is even more characteristic and certainly more famous for mingling comic and serious choruses in a cycle of considerable magnitude. Sentimental characters emerge from Vecchi's music; and funny episodes, such as a sabbath in the ghetto, carry the old madrigal technique to an extreme and final point.

Orazio Vecchi's last years in Modena were full of strange violence which could not all have been caused by his fascinating and often provocative individuality. One night, "a hore 22" on 5 February 1594, he was attacked by an assassin but escaped unharmed. The organist of Sant'Agostino quarreled with him openly over questions of liturgy and competence. A pupil whom he had generously sponsored intrigued against him successfully in order to succeed him as choir director at the Duomo. His brother's wife became entangled in an adulterous affair which erupted in a bloody domestic scandal.

We are mentioning these details not for the sensation they create, but because similar incidents seem to be peculiar to several Modena musicians. One does not readily associate composers with bloodshed and scandal. Nevertheless, as one scans the array of composers born in Modena over the centuries, only two (besides Orazio Vecchi) rise above a host of ordinary mediocrities; and, as it happens, their undisputed musical merits are matched by singularly unsavory personal experiences.

Alessandro Stradella was born in Modena in 1642. He was a most original contributor to the early *concerto grosso* and to the early opera buffa. His oratorio *San Giovanni Battista* enjoyed enormous popularity, and English writers were the first to acknowledge Purcell's indebtedness to him. Today his music is hardly played, primarily because most of it has remained in manuscript. Nonetheless, anybody who has ever attended a performance of Handel's *Israel in Egypt* will have heard some good Stradella music; for Handel, happily following the free customs of his time, used long sections of a *Serenata* by Stradella for at least four famous choruses. The flies, lice, and locusts; the hailstones; the pastoral "He led them forth like sheep"; and the weighty closing number of the first part—they are all Handel's transcriptions of a Modena original.

Stradella's personal life was so romantic that it served another opera composer for a libretto. Next to *Martha, Alessandro Stradella* is Von Flotow's most popular work; it reached New York in 1853 in less than a decade after its Hamburg premiere. In an oil painting in the Naples conservatory, Stradella looks like a beatnik. Much remains mysterious; but it is established that he eloped with a young girl of the Venetian aristocracy who apparently preferred him to the senator she was supposed to marry. Hired assassins followed the composer from then on. He escaped one attempt on his life in Rome, and legend has it that the murderers' hearts were melted by his music. It is fact, however, that hired gangsters in Turin were more successful in a later attempt. Stradella was barely forty years old at the time of his death.

The other Modena composer of reputation is Giovanni Battista Bononcini, whose typical Baroque output is less remembered than his rivalry with Handel. The details, although not bloody, are nasty and too much conditioned by the local situation to be easily comprehended today. The fact is that Bononcini and Handel vied for the favor and box-office money of London society and audiences; and although the desire to outdo each other in Italianate operas written for English audiences may have been praiseworthy, the means employed were not. The historians Hawkins, who knew both, was fair to write that Bononcini's style "was tender, elegant, and pathetic. Handel's had all these qualities, and numberless others, and his invention was inexhaustible." But the contest became a political issue that split leading families of the London aristocracy. Theater agents added fuel to the flame by competing for houses, productions, and singers. One entrepreneur even managed to get an opera on the stage during the 1721–22 season in which one act was written by Bononcini and one by Handel. The artistic conflict between the two composers turned from a sensation to a scandal when tracts were circulated with accusations of cheat and fraud. The faction behind the Modena composer eventually gave up. One wonders why the accusation of plagiarism should have harmed its candidate when one remembers that Handel, no different from his contemporaries, openly utilized a Bononcini aria in his *Judas Maccabaeus* ("Sion now her head shall raise").

In any case, Bononcini fell in disgrace. He lost his money with his reputation. Then he attached himself to a swindler who professed to have the secret of manufacturing gold. The last decades of his life were restless, miserable, and obscure.

Without wishing to overstress a point, we note in Modena one more conspicuous connection of music with bloodshed. The oldest musical document in the city (identified in the cathedral library as Codex O.I.4) is the *Canto delle Scolte Modenesi,* a song of the local militia allegedly composed during the threat of a Hungarian invasion in 899.

Otherwise one must not forget that the quarter-million volumes of the Biblioteca Estense in the Palazzo dei Musei include extraordinary compositions of many centuries. The music collection in Modena has remained rare and rich, even after family politics in the early nineteenth century removed much of it to the Austrian National Library in Vienna.

NAPLES

NEAPOLITAN OPERA is not so much a geographic as a technical term. Just as a Vienna classical symphony, for instance, denotes not an Austrian attribute but a musical structure, so a Neapolitan opera refers not to a local enterprise but to a basic conviction. One of the fundamental problems in an opera is the relation of music to the other arts. The founders of opera around 1600 in Florence, with their own view of Greek drama, subordinated the music completely to the text and the action. The entire subsequent history of opera can be represented as a pendulum swinging from one extreme to the other. The purely musical needs could never be suppressed for long. But whenever the music seemed to get out of hand, so to speak, favoring trills and high *C*'s for their own sake at the expense of dramatic expression and diction, someone was sure to initiate an opera reform by remembering (and usually misinterpreting) the function of the classic Greek drama.

In this idealistic light, the efforts of Gluck and Wagner can be understood as variations and amplifications of the theme set by the Florentine *camerata*. Their respective reforms did not restore Greek drama, but the unexpected results showed a merit of their own. The Gluck reform set out to halt the whim and vanity of singers who had mercilessly tried to dominate the taste of opera composers through much of the eighteenth century. Wagner's concept of the universal artwork necessarily removed music from the exalted role allotted to it by the preceding generation of composers like Rossini. If the late operas of Monteverdi, Mozart, and Verdi have been singled out as uniquely superior specimens, one criterion for this deserved evaluation is doubtless the ingenious manner in which these masters, each in his own way, reconciled the demands of the music with those of the drama.

In this swing of the pendulum between musical subservience and musical autonomy, Neapolitan opera occupies the extreme position of the latter. Reacting to the initial dramatic concerns of the Florentine *camerata* around 1600, the musical forces slowly asserted their rights. In Naples, the man in the street likes to sing. It was inevitable that, sooner or later, he would put himself on the stage. By the year 1700, and for the next few generations, composers, particularly in Naples, gained success and popularity by sacrificing the structure and literary demands of an opera to a series of tuneful arias. This sensuous pleasure and faith in the human voice is probably the most distinct feature of Neapolitan opera. If one wishes, one may make nice differentiations between aristocratic and democratic operas, polyphonic and homophonic, learned and frivolous, elegant and folksy, *seria* and *buffa.* They vary in regard to technique and plot; but whether mythological heroes or Neapolitan chambermaids were involved, in eighteenth-century Naples arias alone defined the nature and fate of an opera. There were arias suiting each desired expression: tender, lamenting, dignified, pathetic, agitated, facile. Sparkling above all these types was the aria *di bravura* which permitted a singer to indulge in agile ornamentation and to display the powers and compass of the voice. As a result, Neapolitan opera became a singer's paradise in which he more often than not considered the composer an inferior supplier of a minimal outline.

This kind of musician's opera spread all over Europe, but it is appropriately called "Neapolitan," not only because the first composers associated with it practiced in Naples, but because the essential quality of reveling in the sound of a human voice is as typically Neapolitan as *Lacrima Christi.*

Before concentrating on the Real Teatro di San Carlo, the glorious tangible monument to opera in Naples, we might think of two singers who by a span of two thousand years between them add an element of timelessness to the Neapolitan scene.

Enrico Caruso, a legendary phenomenon by now, was born in Naples in 1873. As the nineteenth child of a poor laborer, he could count on neither money nor leisure for voice lessons. He really taught himself how to sing. His superior craft, by all reports, grew out of his enormous power of concentration, his acute ear, and his attentive self-criticism; yet one is willing to assume that a Neapolitan attitude in and around him participated in his formation. When he appeared at the San Carlo in 1901 after establishing his fame elsewhere, the audience, for whatever reason, showed so little enthusiasm for his Nemorino and Des Grieux (Massenet) that he swore never to sing in Naples again. He returned in 1921 to die, and his embalmed body in full dress was seen for eight years in the cemetery of Del Planto—which is located today between the airport and the city—until his widow, by a direct appeal to the government, had the glass sarcophagus closed.

Another singer began his stage career in Naples after having studied music in Rome. Because he wanted to strengthen his naturally feeble and husky voice, "he would lie on his back with a slab of lead on his chest, use enemas and emetics to keep down his weight, and refrain from eating apples and every other food considered deleterious to the vocal cords." When he felt that he had made sufficient progress, the Emperor Nero chose Naples over Rome for his stage debut in the year 64, when he was twenty-seven years old. The historian Suetonius reports that he sang his aria through to the end, disregarding an earthquake which destroyed the theater shortly after the performance. Nero often returned to Naples, either (unlike Caruso) to sing himself or to drink and dine in the orchestra. In Naples he also taught a specially selected claque of more than five thousand youths the Alexandrian method of applause: humming like bees, clapping with hands hollowed like roof tiles, and beating the flat hands like brickbats.

The collapse of a theater has never deterred the Neapolitans from building a new one. The Teatro di San Carlo is only one among many in which singers have wooed local audiences. But it is one of the most spectacular halls anywhere and, moreover, the domicile of the oldest autonomous opera company in Italy. The present building was opened in 1817 after the original structure of 1737 had burned down—as the result not of an earthquake but of a lantern left aglow on the stage after a ballet rehearsal. The San Carlo easily offers the most satisfactory opera experience in Italy, combining the qualitative efforts of the Teatro alla Scala in Milan with the noble elegance of the Teatro La Fenice in Venice (two analogies that must not be reversed). But even out of season, the traveler should strive for admission to the white-and-gold auditorium, which is no more strenuous to gain and no less rewarding to behold than the crater of Vesuvius.

The traveler, more than the native, will be interested in finding an Englishman among the long row of general managers. Signor Giuseppe Glossop, *inglese,* originally a tallow chandler who loved the theater, had advanced a large sum toward the construction of the Coburg, now the Old Vic, Theatre in London in 1818. Six years later he took on the opera season at the San Carlo, in addition to that at La Scala. He lasted only a short time, but in his two years in Milan he sponsored close to 250 opera performances by Rossini alone. His grandson, Augustus Henry Glossop must have inherited some Neapolitan traits: managing the Royal Opera House at

Covent Garden at the end of the nineteenth century, he inaugurated what Desmond Shawe-Taylor has called the "age of great singers" in London, Bernard Shaw's complaints notwithstanding.

In both Naples and Milan, Joseph Glossop was succeeded by Domenico Barbaia, who shaped the character of the Teatro di San Carlo as decisively as Gustav Mahler, for instance, shaped that of the Vienna Opera. When he became the impresario of the San Carlo in 1810, he had behind him a career as a circus manager and a coffeehouse waiter. A lasting monument to his inventiveness, along with the fame of the San Carlo, is a coffee or chocolate drink with whipped cream and beaten egg white, called a *barbaiata* in Milan until this day. Money had come his way more quickly than literacy; and Neapolitans circulated the story that to a conductor who complained at a rehearsal about a missing *B*-flat, he threw a purse with the suggestion to go out and buy one. For the next thirty years, off and on, he directed the San Carlo with musical taste and discriminating judgment, reconciling both with the healthy financial sense of an entrepreneur. Rossini was his great friend and money-maker; but at Naples, Barbaia also produced Gluck and Spontini, and introduced Donizetti and Bellini.

While being the impresario of the San Carlo in Naples, Barbaia also was in charge of the Teatro alla Scala in Milan and of the two Vienna opera theaters, at the Kärnthnerthor and an der Wien, so that for two seasons, from 1826 to 1828, he actually managed the opera affairs of three major cities simultaneously, without the benefit of an airplane. He was responsible for the world premiere of Rossini's *Otello* in Naples, Weber's *Euryanthe* in Vienna, and Bellini's *Norma* in Milan —"one of the most fantastic figures," in the words of the Rossini biographer Francis Toye, "in the whole fantastic world of Italian opera."

There is historic justification in the appearance of a

superior impresario in the wake, and not at the head, of a musical drive. Neapolitan opera as a type had experienced its heyday in the century into which Domenico Barbaia was born but which ended when he was only twenty-two. He capitalized on a climate in which opera flourished as the most popular entertainment in town. The performances lasted from eight to midnight. The boxes were comfortable and lighted so that card games, conversations, and dinners could accompany the singers. The alternation of chess and arias was considered marvelously beneficial to both by Charles de Brosses, who had arrived from Burgundy in 1739 to excavate Herculaneum. The Mozarts, too, in May and June of 1770, spent their free evenings attending operas in the Teatro di San Carlo; and the boy reported with glee, not only on composers and singers, but also on the rough Neapolitan upbringing of the king, who in the opera house always stood on a stool so as to appear a little taller than the queen.

The audiences insisted on new works. It has been tabulated that the forty leading Neopolitan composers alone wrote about two thousand operas in the eighteenth century, a fraction of the total output. Alessandro Scarlatti stands at the beginning, having immigrated from Palermo and letting his Naples-born son Domenico depart for nonoperatic pastures. The flow of opera composers in and out of the city continued with such strength that one Michele Alfeltro advised the king of the economic importance of this migration and concluded that it would be wise for the government to make the care of music its responsibility. Indeed, the opera composers in most European centers were Neapolitan by birth, by training, or by style. Neapolitan opera was represented in England by Bononcini and Handel, in Germany by Jommelli and Hasse, in Vienna by Caldara, and in Venice by Gasparini and Vivaldi. Of the multitude active in Naples, the names of Pergolesi, Paisiello, and Cimarosa will be singled out as the only ones still in the regular repertoire. For even if the Teatro di San Carlo occasionally revives a Spontini opera, the scheduling is likely to be the result of local pride in an anniversary rather than of the life of the score.

Giovanni Battista Pergolesi's *La Serva Padrona* has preserved its vitality until today. One must not forget that the audience that first heard it in 1733 (three years before the composer died at the age of twenty-six) recognized the characters as drawn from the contemporary city and the melodies from the patter of the local inflection. *La Serva Padrona* was not considered a full-fledged opera but an intermezzo—a farce to be played, according to Neapolitan custom and appetite, between the acts of a long opera. In all these respects, the Pergolesi work is a representative of its genre and of the city.

Giovanni Paisiello began and ended his long life in the south of Italy, but he spent eight years of his prime in St. Petersburg (now Leningrad) as conductor, inspector, and composer of operas for Empress Catherine the Great. There he wrote and first produced his *Barber of Seville* in 1782, of such impact that Rossini's try at the same libretto thirty-three years later was first considered audacious and unworthy of success. In Paisiello's operas, more than in those of any other Neapolitan, the proximity of Mozart becomes audible.

When Paisiello left St. Petersburg for home, another Neapolitan, the son of a mason and a laundress, took his place at the Russian court in 1787. But Domenico Cimarosa did not like the cold climate. His relief at reaching Vienna on his return trip must have been great; for there he wrote his best work, the opera buffa *Il Matrimonio Segreto,* which is good fun even on the modern stage. Mozart had died in Vienna a few months earlier, and his rival Salieri had abandoned the music direction at the court. Leopold II appointed Cimarosa *Hofkapellmeister,* and it is reported that the emperor requested an immediate repetition of *Il Matrimonio Segreto* after the first hearing. Yet one can understand that the composer preferred to return soon to his native Naples, where his new opera was repeated sixty-seven times in the first season. But a few years later, in 1799, he had—for a composer—the rare experience of being condemned to death for showing too much elation about the Neapolitan revolt against his Bourbon employer. The same republican uprising also damaged the Teatro di San Carlo. As it happened, Cimarosa was pardoned by the royal opera fan; and a public appeal for funds closed the holes in the opera house caused by cannonballs.

For the last thirty-six years of the century, Sir William Hamilton was the English ambassador to Naples. His house became a gathering point not only for politicians but even more for scientists, scholars, and artists. The British Museum now owns many items of his collection. Of the numerous travelers who have published journals about that place and period, hardly any fail to mention Sir William's intelligent and sensitive hospitality. Every English schoolboy knows the story of his second wife's affair with Admiral Nelson. Goethe met her in Naples shortly after her arrival and expressed pleasure that Hamilton, "a person of universal taste," had "found rest at last in a most beautiful wife, the masterpiece of the great Artist." It was the first Lady Hamilton, however, who helped arrange a concert for the boy Mozart in the spring of 1770. She was a neat and expressive pianist herself; and father Mozart, who knew her from London, reported with great satisfaction that she trembled when asked to play for his son.

The Neapolitan predilection for sounds (to which the incessant noise on the streets, now as then, may well be related) would not have sufficed to produce musically significant works if the native instincts had not been trained in disciplined channels. Naples was renowned for its four conservatories, the origins of which went back to the sixteenth century. These music schools, originally founded as institutions in which orphans taken out of the streets were taught ecclesiastical music, became models of their kind for all of Europe in the seventeenth and eighteenth centuries. Most of the Neapolitan opera composers were connected with one or the other conservatory—as students or teachers or both. The original buildings of Santa Maria di Loreto, Sant'Onofrio a Capuana, Poveri di Gesù Cristo, and Pietà de' Turchini in the course of time were put to other uses—barracks, hospital, seminary, monastery.

The present Conservatorio di Musica is the collective heir of the four older conservatories. Since 1826 it has been attached to the austere Gothic church building of San Pietro a Maiella on the Via dei Tribunali, a few blocks south of the Museo Nazionale. After the completion of the current renovation, the permanent exhibition of the conservatory promises to amuse and instruct the inquiring visitor. Otherwise only the stone walls convey an idea of the former conservatory atmosphere. Boarders are no longer taken in, the students do not wear distinctly colored uniforms, and the emerging sounds are not distinguishable from similar ones in conservatories across the United States. But when the Irish boy Michael Kelly (who later sang Mozart's first Basilio) arrived in 1779 to be admitted as a paying student to the Conservatorio di Santo Onofrio, he became so frightened by the terrific noise that he fled into the isolation of private lessons.

This is Dr. Burney's description of the scene, dated Wednesday, 31 October 1770: "This morning I went with young Oliver to his Conservatorio of St. Onofrio, and visited all the rooms where the boys practise, sleep, and eat. On the first flight of stairs was a trumpeter, screaming upon his instrument till he was ready to burst; on the second was a french-horn, bellowing in the same manner. In the common practising room there was a *Dutch concert,* consisting of seven or eight harpsichords, more than as many violins, and several voices, all performing different things, and in different keys: other boys were writing in the same room; but it being holiday time, many were absent who usually study and practise there together.

"The jumbling them all together in this manner may be convenient for the house, and may teach the boys to attend to their own parts with firmness, whatever else may be going forward at the same time; it may likewise give them force, by obliging them to play loud in order to hear themselves; but in the midst of such jargon, and continued dissonance, it is wholly impossible to give any kind of polish or finishing to their performance; hence the slovenly coarseness so remarkable in their public exhibitions; and the total want of taste, neatness, and expression in all these young musicians, till they have acquired them elsewhere.

"The beds, which are in the same room, serve as seats for the harpsichords and other instruments. Out of thirty or forty boys who were practising, I could discover but two that were playing the same piece: some of those who were practising on the violin seemed to have a great deal of hand. The violoncellos practise in another room: and the flutes, hautbois, and other wind instruments, in a third, except the trumpets and horns, which are obliged to fag, either on the stairs, or on the top of the house.

"There are in this college sixteen young *castrati,* and these live up stairs, by themselves, in warmer apartments than the other boys, for fear of colds, which might not only render their delicate voices unfit for exercise at present, but hazard the entire loss of them for ever.

"The only vacation in these schools, in the whole year, is in autumn, and that for a few days only: during the winter, the boys rise two hours before it is light, from which time they continue their exercise, an hour and a half at dinner excepted, till eight o'clock at night; and this constant perseverance, for a number of years, with genius and good teaching, must produce great musicians."

Just behind the Conservatorio di Musica San Pietro a Maiella, a drama was enacted by a composer—not on a stage, but in the palace he inhabited. Don Carlo Gesualdo, Prince of Venosa, killed his adulterous wife and her lover in the Palazzo Sansevero at No. 9 on the Piazza San Domenico Maggiore. Today the gloomy building contains about fifty apartments; and Gesualdo's crime has apparently been forgiven by the new admirers of his daring (and somewhat dilettantish) harmonic progressions. A huge painting depicting the murder can be seen in the Capuchin monastery at Gesualdo, about forty-five miles east of Naples, which he founded in expiation of his violent deed. Gesualdo commissioned the architect Cosimo Fanzago to design a chapel in the church of Gesù Nuovo, the third on the left. In the floor before this chapel, the princely criminal composer was buried in 1613. So far he has not found much peace; for the tombstone was destroyed by an earthquake in 1688 and damaged by a bomb in 1943, a reverential restoration following each disaster. The Baroque organ cases in both Gesù Nuovo and San Domenico Maggiore are too excessive to be overlooked by anyone tracing the Gesualdo mementos in this quarter of Naples.

The sensuous satisfaction in sound, so typical of Naples, has found forms that have lasted across the centuries. The Pompeian mosaic of the street musicians in the Museo Nazionale in Naples may be small; but just as it attracts considerable attention today for its artistic merit, so it enjoyed popularity (confirmed by copies) in antiquity. One finds it in the left wing of the mezzanine. While the eye can trace the movements of the dancers, the ear must fancy the noise made by the stamping feet, the tambourine, the cymbals, the voices of the two ballad-singing men, the double pipes, and the unidentified instrument held by the boy. This scene presented by a troupe of street musicians must have been a common sight in the city two thousand years ago; and, with variants of detail, it is still today.

But there are aural relics as well. In the central and congested quarter of Montecalvario, the faithful are called to a religious procession on the twelve Marian Saturday nights (from the beginning of September to that of December) with a chant that betrays its antique Greek origin by a now obsolete scale (in the hypodoric mode). Also in the waning year, on 7 and 8 September, the church of Santa Maria di Piedigrotta becomes the center of a gay feast. There, in the foothills at the western end of town, near the traditional tomb of Virgil, large crowds gather in honor of the Holy Virgin. The form of the celebration gives credence to the suggestion that the holiday long ago initiated the vintage season. Costumed, torchlit multitudes give vent to their musical energy in strangely asymmetrical but strophic folk songs; and to the strumming of guitar and mandolin are added the characteristic rhythms and uncertain pitches of such primeval and otherwise disused instruments as the *putipù, triccaballacche,* and *scetavajasse.*

An experience recorded by Goethe may serve to increase our acoustical tolerance to Naples. He was returning from a trip to Paestum, driving a light two-wheeled carriage with a friend beside him and a rough, good-natured Italian boy behind. "We now reached an eminence; the most extensive view opened before us. Naples in all its splendor, its mile-long line of houses on the flat shore of the bay, the promontories, tongues of land, walls of rock, then the islands, and behind all the sea—the whole was an entrancing sight.

"A most hideous singing or rather exulting crying and joyful howling from the boy behind frightened and disturbed me. Angrily I called out to him; he had never heard any harsh words from us, he had been a very good boy.

"For a while he did not move; then he patted me lightly

on the shoulder, and pushing between us both his right arm, with the forefinger stretched out, exclaimed: *Signor, perdonate! questa è la mia patria!* This means translated: 'Forgive me, Sir, but that is my native land!' And so I was surprised a second time. Something like a tear rose in the eyes of me, the poor northerner!"

ORVIETO

AFTER THE SACK of Rome in 1527, Pope Clement VII found refuge in Orvieto for six months; and the indebtedness of the Roman Catholic Church to the city has been openly recognized. Similar acknowledgment is due a musical incident initiated in Orvieto which involved the survival, not of a person, but of church music.

At the sessions in 1562 of the Council of Trent, the role of music in the liturgy absorbed the attention of the delegates. A considerable faction was apprehensive that polyphonic, i.e., elaborate, settings of the Mass could not "reach tranquilly into the ears and hearts of those who hear them." If music obscured the sacred words, some cardinals concluded, then one should ban from the service all seductive and impure melodies, all outcries and uproars, vocal and instrumental, so that "the House of God may in truth be called a House of prayer." A special commission of cardinals was appointed to examine Masses and to determine whether contrapuntal compositions were really inimical to the glory of God. If this empirical approach eventually led to a toleration of *good* polyphonic compositions in the church, the *magister capellae,* cathedral organist, and town carillonneur of Orvieto had much to do with this decision favorable to music.

The Signorelli frescoes in the Duomo had been in place half a century when Jacobus de Kerle arrived in Orvieto from his native Ypres, in West Flanders, as a young man—probably first as a singer in the cathedral with the additional obligation of training the choir. He made a quick career. Being not only an excellent composer but also a good Catholic—he became an ordained priest in Italy—he was concerned lest an unwise decision in Trent deprive him, and all Roman Catholic congregations, of the satisfaction of harmonizing his religion with his art. In the crucial winter of 1561–62 he composed in Orvieto, and published in Venice, a collection of ten special prayers for the good outcome of the Council, *Preces Speciales Pro Salubri Generalis Concilii.* He quickly sent them to Trent with a personal address to five select cardinals. The dedication alone reveals Kerle's intent to save polyphonic music for the Church. He refers to the sanctity of the text; relates his music to the praises of God and to the time of the Church; appeals to the wisdom and taste of the legates; names King David as an ally and a precedent; and expresses the devout wish that his plan of composition would please the Council. The *Preces Speciales* were repeatedly sung for the delegates, and indeed they pleased. Kerle had been singularly purposeful in treating the words with care and the music with economy. The Council found the *Preces* edifying and timely and applauded them generously. Jacobus de Kerle doubtless influenced the decision of the special music commission to retain contrapuntal music in the Roman Catholic liturgy; yet he never sacrificed his high artistic to his serious religious convictions. For demonstrating artistic initiative and courage, the title "savior of music," it has been forcefully suggested, belongs to him rather than to Giovanni Pierluigi da Palestrina, who jumped on a bandwagon.

In the same year, 1562, Kerle left Orvieto for the private chapel of a well-wishing cardinal in Rome. He followed his patron to Barcelona, received through him an excellent position in Augsburg, and spent the eight years before his death in 1591 in the emperor's service in Prague.

Kerle probably had a good organ at his disposal in the

cathedral of Orvieto; for an instrument hanging above the Cappella del Corporale, the same location as that of the modern organ, is documented as early as 1373. The beautiful Baroque case visible today was, however, installed in 1582 shortly after his departure. Famous in the seventeenth century for an abundance of flute stops—perhaps a Sicilian influence, although the builder Vincenzo Fulgenzi was Flemish—the organ today contains almost exclusively new pipes which speak forcefully whenever they are not muted by the bats nesting in them. An exception is the front row where some of the biggest pipes have survived intact since the end of the sixteenth century. The largest of them in the center is 26¾ feet long and weighs 321 pounds.

There are many other musical instruments in the cathedral which promise to burst into sound on the Day of Judgment. Signorelli's frescoes associate bliss with music. The preponderance of stringed instruments in his vision of paradise reflects a truth that is deeper than mere convention. The ancient Greeks considered the stringed instruments sacred, appertaining to the god of light, Apollo, and appropriate to religious services; whereas wind instruments were lascivious, invented by barbarians, and admissible only at secular entertainments. Metal instruments in all civilizations have been attributed to subterranean creators, rough and ugly like Hephaestus and Alberich; and to pitiless users, destructive and violent like Joshua and Gabriel. Ovid speaks of metal as the root of evil, and of "the guilt of iron, and gold, more guilty still." Anyone doubting that this appraisal is deeply engrained in us need only ponder how a church congregation would respond to the sound of a saxophone or trumpet during the service as compared to that of a violin or violoncello. When Signorelli filled his paradise with stringed instruments, he passed a moral judgment on musical instruments which has become legalized by the Roman Catholic Church.

PADUA

UNDER THE SEVEN CUPOLAS of the basilica of Sant'Antonio one should give thought to a musician whose work provided a fair match for the visual splendor of the building. Giuseppe Tartini and the city of Padua acted strongly upon each other. In 1713, when he was twenty-one years old and a student at the university, he eloped with one of his violin pupils who belonged to the family of Cardinal Giorgio Cornaro. The cardinal showed his disapproval of the marriage by ordering Tartini's arrest. The musician fled Padua and spent the next two years disguised as a monk in Assisi. There he demonstrated that acoustics and music are good mates by discovering difference tones (the phenomenon of a third tone heard by the ear when two loud tones are sounded together); by thickening the strings on the violin; and by redesigning and lightening the bow. In Assisi he also wrote a sonata which, more than any other of his several hundred compositions, has carried his fame into the modern concert hall. This is Tartini's own account of the creation of the "Devil's Trill" Sonata:

"One night I dreamt that I had made a bargain with the devil for my soul. Everything went at my command; my novel servant anticipated every one of my wishes. Then the idea suggested itself to hand him my violin to see what he would do with it. Great was my astonishment when I heard him play, with consummate skill, a sonata of such exquisite beauty as surpassed the boldest flights of my imagination. I felt enraptured, transported, enchanted; my breath failed me, and—I awoke. Seizing my violin I tried to reproduce the sounds I had heard. But in vain. The piece I then composed, 'The Devil's Sonata,' although the best I ever wrote, how far was it below the one I had heard in my dream!"

In Assisi, Tartini also attracted crowds to the Franciscan service by his extraordinary violin playing. When some Paduan pilgrims in 1715 heard the exquisite music while paying homage to the Saint and realized what they had lost in Tartini, the cardinal's severe opposition melted; and the fiddler was permitted to return to his home in Padua. We can infer the excellence of his playing from his appointment to the post of first violin at the Cappella del Santo when he was not quite twenty-nine years old. The music organization at the basilica of Sant'Antonio then numbered sixteen singers and twenty-four instrumentalists, and membership in this elite group was determined by strict annual examinations. But in the case of "Signor Giuseppe Tartini, an extraordinary violinist," any proof of his mastery was waived. A good salary and various personal privileges indicated Padua's esteem for the musician and helped keep him content in town until his death in 1770, a half century later.

Tartini's loyalty to Sant'Antonio is all the more remarkable as the capitals of Europe vied for his presence. Prague was passionately stirred after hearing him at the coronation of Emperor Charles VI. London and Paris repeatedly failed to changed his conviction that "the skin is nearer than the purse," work in Padua more satisfying than riches elsewhere. Naples literally carried him around town; and Rome heard his *Miserere,* composed at the personal request of the Pope, on Ash Wednesday in the Sistine Chapel. Rather than satisfying his vanity by commercial concerts, Tartini preferred relaying his knowledge and craft to deserving students. He founded a school of violin playing at Padua; and when he eventually became known as the "Master of Nations," Padua shared his fame by gaining the title of "School of Nations." His pupils came from all parts of the earth and continued his tradition of virtuosity paired with intelligence.

The English musician Dr. Charles Burney regarded it as a particular misfortune that he arrived in Padua half a year after Tartini's death, "for he was a professor, whom I was not more desirous to hear perform, than ambitious to converse with." The presence of four organs in the basilica of Santo Antonio (now there is only one) did not fill the gap left by Tartini, particularly as Burney found "that two of the four organs were more than sufficient to over-power the voices."

Tartini is buried, not in the basilica where his violin contributed to the glory of Sant'Antonio, but in the small church of Santa Caterina (on the Via Cesare Battista nearby). His tombstone, which identifies him as Ioseph Tartini, occupies a position of honor between the first pew and the choir fence on the right. A plaque on the outside of the building rightly reminds the visitor that while the church of Santa Caterina guards the tomb of Tartini, the basilica of Sant'Antonio guards his compositions and honors his memory. This statement is verified by a stone tablet in the first cloister of the basilica, and a good bust in the second cloister. The city of Padua, moreover, placed a life-size statue of the musician among the other celebrities in the Prato della Valle.

The traveler who has made the round of this vast park—whether to look at Tartini or to imagine the musical open-air festivities held in the Middle Ages on this site of a former Roman theater—might want to enter the large church of Santa Giustina at the southern end of the Prato. The two organs appear, but do not sound, the same as they did to Wolfgang Amadeus Mozart when he played one of them on 13 March 1771. Father Leopold liked the instrument very much—more, apparently, than whichever of the four organs in

Sant'Antonio his fifteen-year-old son also tried on the one full day they spent in Padua.

Tartini's emphasis on teaching and his preoccupation with the writing of theory books, notwithstanding his excellence as a performer and composer, were in line with a long academic tradition characteristic of Padua. The local university, founded in 1222 in the wake of an exodus of scholars from Bologna, is among the most famous in Europe. In more than just the physical sense, it lies in the center of town. Among its professors have been counted the humanist Bembo, the scientist Galilei, the surgeon Acquapendente; and among its law students, the poet Tasso. The presence of the university increased the attraction of Padua for Giotto and Donatello. Although the university, unlike others in Italy, had no chair of music in the Middle Ages, it encouraged the treatment of music in many ways. The students liked singing and performing then as they do now, and their musical activities were respected as a contribution to the cultural life of the town.

At the beginning of the fourteenth century, Marchettus of Padua established himself as a forceful teacher of music theory, practical in his concern for a fixed notation and very conservative in his appraisal of contemporary music, the *ars nova* of the *trecento*. He was therefore promptly declared unintelligent and compared to an ox by one of his academic successors, Prosdocimus de Beldemandis. This Paduan patrician had studied at the university around the year 1400 and was habilitated as a professor of mathematics and astronomy by 1422. The medieval curriculum, one must remember, contained the seven liberal arts of which the quadrivium of arithmetic, geometry, astronomy, and music provided the advanced contents; and the "trivial" disciplines of grammar, logic, and rhetoric, the methods. A professor of mathematics and astronomy was expected to treat of music; and Prosdocimus de Beldemandis' books include eight on music, of which the library in Padua owns half of the original or copied *quattrocento* manuscripts (the others are in Einsiedeln, Lucca, Rome, and Bologna). His treatises cover the problems of counterpoint and of contemporary French and Italian notation (i.e., practical melodic and rhythmic questions). His division of the octave into seventeen steps (in *De Modo Monochordum Dividendi* of 1413) stamps him as an heir of Pythagoras and an explorer of chromaticism.

PALERMO

PALERMO HAS ALMOST the worst slums, and almost the largest opera stage, of any town in Europe. Only Paris and now Vienna boast of a larger stage. The Teatro Massimo on the Piazza Verdi, on the border between the old and modern sections of the town, might at first glance look familiar to the visitor from New York: the two lions, the wide flight of steps, and a pseudo-Greek portico evoke an image of the Public Library on Fifth Avenue. The Teatro Massimo was built by a local architect who had received the first prize in a public competition announced for the purpose in 1864. The jury was headed by Gottfried Semper, whose ideas on theater construction later helped Wagner build Bayreuth. The passing of time has its own laws in Sicily, it seems. Thirty-three years elapsed —full of polemics, lawsuits, and political intrigues—before the grand opera theater opened in 1897 (with *Falstaff* by Verdi, who was not invited). Another fifty years went by before *Le Nozze di Figaro* introduced a Mozart opera to Sicily as a novelty in the quinquagenary celebrations of 1947. The opening season in 1897 included Ponchielli's *Gioconda* with the twenty-four-year-old Caruso in the role of Enzo.

There had been earlier, smaller opera houses in Palermo —as one might expect of any Italian town—but their history is routine. Donizetti came to the city and conducted a newly composed opera in 1826, *Alahor di Granata*. The greatest musical native son, Alessandro Scarlatti, left for the mainland (first Rome and then Naples) as a young man, like so many a Sicilian today. He was born into a musical family in Palermo in 1660 and has gained everlasting fame by his operas, 115 in all, apart from many compositions in other genres. The Neapolitan opera school, of which he is commonly called the founder, developed a new musical idiom that eventually was perfected by Mozart and Rossini. Alessandro was the father of Domenico Scarlatti, his son already born in Naples and more familiar to members of our society through his exquisite piano sonatas.

In the winter of 1881–82, Richard Wagner stayed at the luxurious Hotel des Palmes on the Via Roma (now Grande Albergo e Delle Palme). Working on the completion of *Parsifal,* he used a harmonium which is now displayed in a *salone* of the Teatro Massimo. The hotel clerk did not admit Renoir, then forty years old, who had come expressly from Naples to paint Wagner. There were other rebuffs before Wagner consented to see Renoir on 14 January, although he was very tired from putting the finishing touches on the *Parsifal* score. In bad French he agreed to sit for the painter the next day. Renoir was satisfied with the result; the oil painting made from the sketch, now hanging in the Paris Opéra, is in his own words "a small reminder of this marvelous head." But he was aware of the fact that after a half hour his model "lost his humor and became stiff." "I look like a Protestant clergyman," the musician said to the painter.

The artistic glamour of Palermo's past is strongly reflected by rare Greek metopes in the Museo Nazionale, sparkling mosaics in the Cappella Palatina, and the sumptuous royal tombs in the cathedral. Architectural splendor must have been accompanied by appropriate music, which is less in evidence only because it is not built of stone. The Greek temples and theaters scattered over the island all resounded with music in antiquity. Pindar dedicated fifteen victory odes to the

Sicilians, and the names, though not the compositions, of the musicians Empedocles and Theocritus are recorded. The height of medieval Sicilian cultural glamour around 1200, as apparent by the foundation of Monreale, coincides with the activities of the troubadours and minnesingers. One usually thinks about them as poets, but one must not overlook the fact that they sang their verses. Although many of the melodies were improvised and are therefore lost to us, others have been preserved and are rewarding to hear. We know that the Norman King William II kept excellent singers at his Palermo court, but the Hohenstaufens themselves were musicians (a common enough quality among rulers if one remembers the Habsburgs, Henry VIII, Frederick the Great, and also Nero).

Henry VI, whose tomb is in the Palermo Cathedral, was an illustrious minnesinger. Of his son Frederick II the chronicle tells that "legere scribere et cantare sciebat et cantilenas et cantiones invenire." ("He could read, write, and sing, and compose secular and religious songs.") He also invited musicians from Provence and Germany to Palermo. What did the music sound like? The Italian poet and literature professor, Carducci, has an ear for it: "Princes, barons, judges, attorneys in the retinue of Frederick II sang of the joys and sorrows of love with sometimes so ardent a passion that it continues to burn in the ditties of the Sicilian people even today."

PALESTRINA

PALESTRINA IS THE NAME, primarily, of a town and not of a composer. The latter's name was Giovanni Pierluigi. He is by no means a rare—only a famous—case of a man's being identified by his birthplace. One reaches Palestrina from Rome in little more than an hour by train, bus, or car (out the Porta Maggiore). The old hill town, halfway on the road to the gout-curing Fiuggi waters, strikes one as aloof—not only in its isolated location, but just as much in the spirit of its inhabitants. Its great musical son is, of course, known by his family name. The Corso Pierluigi is one of the main streets leading away from the Duomo; and not far from it, on the Via Cecconi, one finds the Casa di Pierluigi, or what is left of it. In the Second World War, an American bomb destroyed all but the walls of the house in which the composer was born in 1525. It must have been a small house but probably solid and respectable in its day.

There are few composers in history about whom more nonsense has been circulated than about Giovanni Pierluigi da Palestrina. Even the current tourist pamphlet published officially by the Ente Provinciale per il Turismo di Roma calls him briefly the "creatore della polifonia," the creator of polyphony. Actually the art of writing several independent melodies against one another—and as such polyphony is one of the great spiritual accomplishments and characteristics of Western civilization—was "created" at least five hundred years before

Palestrina was born. Notre Dame in Paris resounded with four-part compositions by the time of the Crusades around the year 1200. The Netherlands schools, finally, a century before Palestrina, achieved supreme mastery of polyphony in both technical and expressive respects. Like every other musician of his time, Palestrina knew the craft of polyphony. Far from having "created" it, he contributed toward its dissolution at the end of the sixteenth century by adjusting the independent voices of a chorus and accommodating them to one another to such an extent that the result often sounds like a progression of unified chords.

The virtue that lies in this apparent simplicity has given rise to another Palestrina legend, namely, that he "saved" church music from being banished altogether from the Roman Catholic service. The Council of Trent, convening during Palestrina's lifetime in order to stem the revolutionary tide of Protestantism, urged that church music be "purged of all sensual and impure elements, all secular forms and unedifying language." A commission of cardinals examined church music by listening to some of the repertory of the Papal Choir, in which Palestrina was represented. The cardinals seemed satisfied that the music was pure (i.e., not experimental and complex) and edifying (because the simultaneous movement of the voices made the holy words intelligible). Inevitably and immediately, church composers like Giovanni Animuccia at St. Peter's in Rome and Vincenzo Ruffo at the Duomo in Milan declared their willingness to conform to the rules of the Tridentine Council; and Palestrina was no less opportunistic when stating in the preface to his second book of Masses in 1567 that he was endeavoring to write "music of a new order, in accordance with the views of the most serious and religious-minded personages in high places."

Apart from all fables, his greatness need not be disputed. He wrote almost one hundred Masses and about six hundred liturgical motets, not to mention smaller secular pieces. Across the centuries one admires the long breath of his phrases and the calm sonority of his expression. Nevertheless, in this hill town where he was born and where as a young man he played the organ and directed the choir at the cathedral, the lesson is worth remembering that artistic supremacy and systematic opportunism are not always incompatible. He married rich, twice. When his first wife died as one of the ten thousand victims of the pestilence in Rome, he very suddenly and emphatically decided to become a priest—partly, no doubt, to strengthen his position in the Papal Chapel, from which an earlier Pope, Paul IV, had fired him on the legal grounds that he was a layman. But before taking the final vow, he suddenly —within eight months after burying his first wife—married a rich widow and became her partner in a lucrative fur and leather business. He ran the business for at least a decade, investing in it money he had borrowed from his wife at the usurer's rate of 8 percent. During this period (he was about sixty years old), he intrigued with singers of the Papal Choir against their director, whose position he had long coveted. The intrigue was discovered; the ringleaders were suspended; and Palestrina, though otherwise honored in Rome and famous as far as Germany and England, never gained the title which he craved.

On the whole, his career was very successful. After leaving Palestrina in 1551, he composed and performed in Rome in succession at St. Peter's, the Sistine Chapel, San Giovanni in Laterano, Santa Maria Maggiore, and finally again at St. Peter's—all the "best" churches, as it were, in Papal Rome. In line with his character, it is worth mentioning that his first appointment to the distinguished pontifical choir—by Julius III, who had been Bishop of Palestrina—was "by order of our lord the pope, without examination, and without the assent of the singers"; that he resigned from St. John Lateran abruptly after refusing to meet some of his financial obligations to the choristers; that he turned down, by demanding an exorbitant salary, the most honorific offer a composer could then receive: to take charge of the music at the court of the Holy Roman Emperor Maximilian II in Vienna; that he did not mind quitting the church service altogether when summer employment at the Villa d'Este in Tivoli seemed to bring more money and pleasure; and that he played a salary offer from Santa Maria Maggiore against one from St. Peter's until he secured a maximum bid from the latter. None of these transactions need detract from the intrinsic value of his music. When the Caligula obelisk was erected in the Piazza San Pietro in 1586, Giovanni Pierluigi da Palestrina marched at the head of the Papal Choir which was singing his setting of the text *O crux ave, spes unica* for the occasion.

When he was almost seventy, he decided to relinquish his eminent post at St. Peter's, the center of Christendom, for the modest position that he had held at the beginning of his career —that of organist and choir director at the cathedral of Palestrina, where the house of his family was still standing. His death in 1594 prevented him from completing the cycle.

PARMA

ON 13 MAY 1944, an American bomb exploded on the top floor of the Palazzo della Pilotta, which the Farnese family had built around the year 1600. The various museums housed in the palace managed somehow to preserve their treasures; but the Teatro Farnese, on the same level with the Galleria Nazionale, was shattered into fragments. Work to restore the theater has been in progress for some time but is far from complete.

The traveler will be well rewarded if he turns right before entering the picture gallery. One such traveler was, even in the early postwar years when a guide, persuaded by a sentimental plea as much as by a bank note, and rightly concerned that parts of the ceiling might yet come down on the visitor's head, unlocked the door to the theater. The proportions of the long room have remained more memorable than the clouds of dust that enveloped him and the legion of wooden statues laid out like corpses.

The beauty, function, and success of Palladio's wooden Teatro Olimpico in Vicenza, which had opened in 1585, prompted the proud Farnese rulers of Parma to send the architect Giovanni Battista Aleotti to Vicenza to inspect, apply, and preferably surpass, the olympic model. Palladio's theater is the only one of its kind that has survived intact until today. The Teatro Farnese, even as a reconstructed ruin, shows both Aleotti's respect for the older master and his reliance on his own imagination. The visual impression will prove both points. Whoever misses the fixed-scene perspective of the Teatro Olimpico should be reminded that the Teatro Farnese had grooves for sliding wings and machinery for quick changes of scenery and for spectacular histrionics.

According to a letter from an eyewitness, the Teatro Farnese might easily have been turned into ruins by the events of the opening night on 21 December 1628, without waiting three hundred years for a bomb. The new duke, Odoardo Farnese, was marrying Margherita de' Medici, Cosimo II's daughter. Opera may have been born in Florence three decades earlier, but now in Parma it would be bigger and better. Monteverdi—by then firmly established in Venice and associated with the new art form combining music, poetry, and action—was invited to come to the Teatro Farnese and provide the music for the wedding show, *Mercurio e Marte*. The music has been lost, but we know that the bridegroom himself and a troupe of horses joined the gigantic cast. Mercury and Mars fought with sea monsters over the fate of the heroes and lovers. Neptune's tide, flooding the arena to the depth of two feet, was finally allayed by Jupiter, who descended from above in a machine with a retinue of a hundred. The Florentine eyewitness, reporting back to the secretary of the Grand Duke, felt mostly fear that the theater would collapse, because in addition to the machines, the performers, and an audience of four thousand, "il medesimo salone avesse anche a sostenere il peso dell'acqua, la quale si alzò meglio di un mezzo braccio" ("the hall had also to sustain the weight of the water which rose more than a half yard").

Although Monteverdi wrote another ballet, *La Vittoria d'Amore* for the Teatro Farnese in 1641, the character of the opening night seems to have predetermined that of future productions. The musical accomplishments were on the whole ephemeral, the spectacles and expenses enormous. But the Teatro Farnese had long periods of silence even in the century following its construction; since 1732 no performance has taken place in it.

That was the year the Farnese were replaced by the Bourbons, the Teatro Farnese by a number of other auditoriums, and Italian opera by French opera. Tommaso Traetta, Gluck's rival and Italian counterpart, spent a few creative years in Parma on his way from Naples to St. Petersburg; and the great Gluck himself was called down from Vienna in 1769 to provide the music for a marriage, in style not unlike that of the early Farnese ventures.

The opera houses that were full of life in eighteenth-century Parma are destroyed, and the musical scores are seldom heard today. But the operatic vitality seems to have flown from the court and the buildings into the population. Parma's passion for opera is proverbial. The tourist will get a whiff of it in his most casual conversations with waiters, hotel clerks, and guides. He will be affected by it inside the Teatro Regio, whether admitted to a performance by a ticket or to the empty house (through a door on the left side) by a tip to the caretaker. Either experience should not be missed.

The Teatro Regio was opened in 1829. The fact that the event turned into a fiasco for *Zaira,* especially commissioned from Bellini, apparently did not prove detrimental to either the composer or the house. Bellini adapted the usable parts of his score for his next opera, *I Capuleti e i Montecchi,* which was successfully performed at the Teatro La Fenice in Venice the following year; and he returned to Parma five years after the opening on the triumphal chariot of *Norma.* The Teatro Regio recovered with three popular Rossini operas, *The Barber of Seville* among them, and has remained healthy and municipally supported until today.

It was built at the initiative of Marie Louise of Habsburg, an ardent music lover like many members of that imperial family. The world outside Parma remembers her mainly as the emperor's daughter forced to marry Napoleon for political reasons; as the faithless wife who abandoned Napoleon when he most needed her in his personal distress; as the negligent mother of *L'Aiglon;* and as the frivolous mistress of Count von Neipperg. In Parma she is remembered as the glamorous ruler whom the Congress of Vienna in 1814 had awarded the duchies of Parma, Piacenza, and Guastalla; as the promulgator of a civil code which gave women equal right to inherit; as a woman of clemency and moderation in the midst of reactionary repression; and as the munificent benefactor of musical institutions.

The Teatro Regio is for the traveler the most appealing monument to Marie Louise's largesse and the musical tradition of the city, but at least two other musical enterprises owe their existence to Marie Louise's initiative.

She founded a school which eventually developed into what is today the Conservatorio di Musica Arrigo Boito. It is housed in an old Carmelite convent with two cool cloisters, rubbing shoulders with elegant Renaissance and Baroque palaces. Among others, Toscanini received his formal training here. As heir to an older tradition, the Conservatorio owns (and readily shows) a well-preserved four-foot positive organ built by Claudio Merulo toward the end of the sixteenth century. This excellent musician, who had played the first organ in San Marco in Venice while Andrea Gabrieli played the second, spent the last two decades of his life in Parma—honored by positions in the Duomo and the church of Santa Maria della Steccata, by performances at court, by the title of *cavaliere* bestowed on him by the duke, Ranuccio Farnese, and by a dignified tomb in the Duomo (near the right side door and the grave of another *cinquecento* composer come from San Marco, Cyprian de Rore).

Among Marie Louise's first acts upon coming to Parma was the establishment of an orchestral association. Two decades later she entrusted Paganini, then at the end and height of his career, with the reform and direction of the orchestra. He had taken violin lessons in Parma as a young boy. Now he hoped for some peace and rest at the Villa Gaione, in the township of Vigatto five miles outside Parma, which he purchased in 1833. The traveler going there by car or taxi will find a spacious country house, now used for religious conferences. A tablet near the entrance recalls the former owner, whose neglect by the city in other respects seems like a continuation of the prejudice manifested against his corpse by the Roman Catholic Church. Paganini was denied ecclesiastical rites and a burial in sacred ground when he died in Nice in 1840, as if the rumors of his pact with the devil were well founded. Five years later, after the punitive verdict of the Bishop of Nice had been revoked by a synodic jury in Genoa, he was temporarily buried in a little chamber, formerly the sacristy, to the left of the altar in the tiny and handsome tenth-century church of Gaione; and a Requiem Mass was celebrated in the church of La Steccata—not for the artist Paganini, but for the Cavalier of the Order of St. George. The transfer to the adjoining cemetery took place in 1853 "in ora notturna" (as we read in the Gaione church register); and only in 1876 did the efforts of his son Achille secure the violinist a final and rather magnificent resting place in the municipal cemetery of Parma (on the first path to the left of the central road, about twenty-five yards from the entrance).

It is opera in the Teatro Regio, without doubt, that continues to set the musical pitch of Parma. While Marie Louise was supervising the construction of the edifice, Giuseppe Verdi was growing up in Busseto, twenty-five miles from the city and within the territory of Parma. The Teatro Regio was seven years old when Verdi completed his first opera, *Oberto, Conte di S. Bonifacio*. He tried to have it performed on his home grounds; but the Teatro Regio, after giving some initial vague promises, returned the score to him as too great a risk, and Verdi's phenomenal operatic career opened at La Scala in Milan. A young English contralto who sang in the premiere, Mary Shaw, wrote home: "We shall be hearing more of him." Parma did, four years and three operas later. *Nabucco,* no risk by that time, was given twenty-two times between 17 April and 28 May 1843. The leading female part of Abigaille was sung by Giuseppina Strepponi, who became Verdi's second wife years later. The initial refusal did not impair the mutual friendship of the city and the composer. The Teatro Regio claims to have produced twenty-three operas of Verdi's total output of twenty-six, probably more than any other opera house. (The stepchildren are *Un Giorno di Regno, Il Corsaro,* and *Stiffelio.*) He, in turn, personally supervised, from the first to the last detail, a history-making *Aida.* He enjoyed the high quality of the *parmigiani* musicians as much as that of the local Lambrusco wine. His devoted admirer Italo Pizzi tells the story of the bass-viol player Pinetti, like Verdi a native of Le Roncole, whom the composer summoned to Milan by wire when a bass-viol player in the orchestra of La Scala criticized a passage as unplayable. The orchestra may have first laughed at the sight of the fat country musician, but when Pinetti ran through the passage with complete ease, Verdi said triumphantly: "That, gentlemen, is how we play in Parma."

Toscanini belonged to this tradition. Already during his lifetime, almost any person asked at random on the street could show the way to the low unmarked house, Borgo Rodolfo Tanzi No. 13, where the maestro was born in 1867. Today the house is identified by a simple plaque. The walk from the Farnese palace across the Verdi bridge (and then left) takes only five minutes, but the neighborhood in the *oltretorrente,* the "wrong side" of the river, has remained physically poor.

Toscanini left Parma as soon as he was graduated from

the conservatory at eighteen. As an advanced student, he played in the opera orchestra of one hundred and twenty musicians, *tutti parmigiani,* which won a contest in 1884 in competition against the orchestras of Turin, La Scala in Milan, Bologna, and Naples. The conductor was Cleofonte Campanini, then twenty-four years old, who succeeded Toscanini as conductor at La Scala. His name is still remembered by opera audiences in Chicago, New York, and London. The Campanini who sang Faust at the opening night of the New York Metropolitan Opera House in 1883 was his older brother Italo, also from Parma.

Toscanini returned to Parma over the years to conduct concerts. It is supreme irony that Parma, of all cities, never heard him conduct an opera.

PESARO

IN TOWNS WHERE there is little to see, reminders must take the place of enduring objects. In Pesaro one should remember that Rossini was born here in 1792 (on the extra day of the leap year). House No. 5 on the street that now bears his name might convey an idea of the physical comfort, or lack of it, available to a family of musicians during the decade when Napoleon invaded Italy. The father was the municipal trumpeter, who earned additional money from the municipality by getting himself appointed inspector of the public slaughterhouses, and from his trumpet by playing in the local theater band. The mother, a baker's only daughter, was a dressmaker who could sing operatic parts without being able to read a note of music. The boy Gioacchino owed very little to Pesaro, for the whole family moved away when he was ten. Moreover, he had been notoriously mischievous.

The traveler might do worse than follow Brahms' example. In May 1888, traveling with a friend from Bologna via Rimini and Ancona to Spoleto and Rome, Brahms did not feel like getting off the train at Pesaro; but in honor of the memory of Rossini, he insisted that each of the travelers sing a melody from the *Barber* right there in the compartment.

RAVELLO

". . . ENCHANTED CASTLE . . . tower . . . stone steps up to the battlemented summit . . . magic garden . . . tropical vegetation, most luxuriant wealth of flowers . . . castle walls . . . abutments . . . florid Arabian style . . . terraces . . . groves . . ."

The visitor to Ravello easily recognizes in this description the Palazzo Rufolo, the strange ruins of Arab-Norman structures from the thirteenth century in the middle of a lush garden. Actually the description is that of the scenery of the second act of Wagner's opera *Parsifal*. The two coincide.

In 1879 Wagner was sixty-six years old. The Bayreuth festival theater had become a reality, and the orchestra sketch for the new opera *Parsifal* was finished. But he suffered from a chronic stomach catarrh, rheumatism, attacks of a painful skin inflammation, insomnia, and fear of a heart attack. The weather that year in his beloved Bayreuth was so depressing that the family decided to spend the winter in Italy. A villa was rented at Posillipo, on the Bay of Naples, and Wagner stayed in Italy from January through October 1880. The scoring of *Parsifal* was temporarily abandoned for a variety of excursions. In May the composer made a trip to Amalfi in the company of a rich young Russian painter, Paul von Joukowsky, who had a studio near Wagner's rented villa and who worshiped the composer. In Ravello they were the guests of an Englishman, Mr. Neville Read, who happened to occupy the Moorish Palazzo Rufolo at the time. If a local guide today claims that Wagner rented the Palazzo, do not believe him. If he offers, however, to show you the rooms while the present aristocrat owner is out, only your northern sense of propriety stands in the way.

Wagner's entry in the visitors' book has been a source of income for the local postcard industry. We read (in German) on a photograph, if not in the original book: "Richard Wagner, with wife and family. Klingsor's magic garden is found! 26 May 1880. R. W." To King Ludwig II of Bavaria, his munificent patron, he wrote: "Here we came upon some splendid suggestions for Klingsor's magic garden: Joukowsky at once made some sketches for the second act of Parsifal . . . We have decided that Joukowsky shall execute detailed designs . . . for the scenery and costumes of Parsifal . . . and as they will be done in exact accordance with my instructions, we may hope to bequeath something really serviceable to posterity."

Later that year in Siena, Joukowsky and Wagner were so impressed by the interior of the cathedral that sketches, made on the spot, were afterward incorporated in the stage setting of the Grail scene.

RAVENNA

IN FRONT OF the mausoleum of Theodoric, outside the Porta Serrata, a tear may be shed to the memory not of the Ostrogoth king but of the musician whom he killed. Boethius, born around 480 in Rome, belonged to an aristocratic family. His education and knowledge synthesized antique and Christian tendencies. He soon caught the attention of King Theodoric, who was ruling the Western Empire from Ravenna. Boethius' theological and philosophical writings, particularly his commentaries on Aristotle, have secured his place in our cultural history. But it has been recorded that King Theodoric called on Boethius' musical experience to find a court musician, as it were, for the Frank King Clovis in 506. Boethius' five volumes *De Institutione Musica* were studied throughout the Middle Ages, which adhered to his classification of music into *musica mundana, musica humana,* and *musica instrumentalis.* For a thousand years he was treated like a kind of musical saint, an absolute authority on matters of music; and when the University of Paris was founded in the thirteenth century, an exact knowledge of Boethius' musical writings became a requirement for the master's degree.

After a life full of political and personal honors, he was appointed *magister officiorum,* administrative head, at the court of Ravenna in 522. Soon thereafter he became entangled in a treason process, although he seems not to have been guilty. The autocratic Theodoric quickly removed his former favorite from all offices, confiscated his goods, held him in jail (where Boethius wrote his famous *Consolation of Philosophy*), and finally had him executed near Pavia in 524.

Theodoric's mausoleum was already standing when Boethius assumed his top position in Ravenna, and the king was buried in it two years after Boethius' death. In the sixteenth and seventeenth centuries, Boethius' tragic end became the topic of many Jesuit dramas.

REGGIO NELL'EMILIA

THE ARTISTIC TEMPERAMENT of this city, less than twenty miles from Parma, has found expression not in any particular building (unless it be the churches) nor in the activity of a creative genius (although Ariosto was born here). It is nonetheless reflected in a century-old passion for the theater. Medieval liturgical dramas, sacred representations, masquerades, comedies, pastorals, musical dramas, operas—they have drawn Reggio citizens in an unbroken tradition to churches, market squares, courtyards, halls, ballrooms, and public theaters.

This atmosphere makes every citizen a musical expert. In the spring of 1872, Mr. Prospero Bertani, who lived in Reggio at Via San Domenico No. 5, initiated the following exchange of letters, which is worth reproducing for the several insights it conveys:

To Giuseppe Verdi Reggio, May 7, 1872

On the second of this month, attracted by the sensation which your opera *Aida* was making, I went to Parma. Half an hour before the performance began I was already in my seat, No. 120. I admired the scenery, listened with great pleasure to the excellent singers, and took pains to let nothing escape me. After the performance was over, I asked myself whether I was satisfied. The answer was in the negative. I returned to Reggio, and on the way back in the railroad carriage, I listened to the verdicts of my fellow travelers. Nearly all of them agreed that *Aida* was a work of the highest rank.

Thereupon I conceived a desire to hear it again, and so on

the fourth I returned to Parma. I made the most desperate effort to obtain a reserved seat, and there was such a crowd that I had to spend five lire to see the performance in comfort.

I came to the following conclusion: the opera contains absolutely nothing thrilling or electrifying, and if it were not for the magnificent scenery, the audience would not sit through it to the end. It will fill the theater a few more times and then gather dust in the archives. Now, my dear Signor Verdi, you can imagine my regret at having spent 32 lire for these two performances. Add to this the aggravating circumstance that I am dependent on my family, and you will understand that this money preys on my mind like a terrible spectre. Therefore I address myself frankly and openly to you, so that you may send me this sum. Here is the account:

Railroad: one way	2.60	lire
Railroad: return trip	3.30	"
Theater	8.00	"
Disgustingly bad dinner at the station	2.00	"
	15.90	lire
Multiplied by 2	x 2	"
	31.80	lire

In the hope that you will extricate me from this dilemma, I am yours sincerely,

BERTANI

Verdi's reply [*addressed to Ricordi*] *May, 1872*

. . . As you may readily imagine, in order to save this scion of his family from the spectres that pursue him, I shall gladly pay the little bill he sends me. Be so kind, therefore, as to have one of your agents send the sum of 27 lire, 80 centesimi to this Signor Prospero Bertani, Via San Domenico No. 5. True, that isn't the whole sum he demands, but for me to pay his dinner too would be wearing the joke a bit thin. He could perfectly well have eaten at home. Naturally, he must send you a receipt, as well as a written declaration that he promises never to hear another one of my new operas, so that he won't expose himself again to the danger of being pursued by spectres, and that he may spare me further travel expenses! [. . .]

May 15, 1872

I, the undersigned, certify herewith that I have received the sum of 27.80 lire from Maestro Giuseppe Verdi, as reimbursement of my expenses for a trip to Parma to hear the opera *Aida.* The Maestro felt it was fair that this sum should be restored to me, since I did not find his opera to my taste. At the same time, it is agreed that I shall undertake no trip to hear any of the Maestro's new operas in the future, unless he takes all the expenses upon himself, whatever my opinion of his work may be.

In confirmation whereof I have affixed my signature,

BERTANI PROSPERO

ROME

EACH TOWN HAS a particular character, and the question whether the character derives from the metaphysical properties of the place or from events and people that form the town's history is fascinating in general but irrelevant to our immediate purpose. The musical life of Florence was social; that of Bologna, academic. The musical life of Rome has the Roman Catholic Church at its source, a few worldly monuments notwithstanding.

Pope Gregory I was the religious and secular ruler of Rome around the year 600. His elevation to sainthood may be traced to his edifying temperament, which suited both his station and his era; his passionate eloquence, which elevated the spirit of his flock; his sense for organization, which seemed to reconcile the present with the future life; and his virtuous care for the purity of the faith. To the musician he has become immortal by his concern for music, and it is proper that the Saint is often represented with a monochord in his hand or a dove near his ear. He had the music of the Church codified by experts; they edited the old Jewish and Greek sources and assimilated the newer Italian traits. The order of the musical liturgy was written down, and Gregorian chant has supplied Western music to this day with a basic vocabulary and an inspired framework.

The extent to which Rome has remained the guardian of church music can be measured by a twentieth-century pronouncement, the *Motu Proprio* of Pope Pius X. If the modern visitor to Rome is to join the millions before him who have entered a church in expectation of a musical as well as spiritual reward, he might well have in mind the principles governing sacred music.

The Roman Catholic Church, while seriously concerned with "maintaining and increasing the beauty of the house of God," is well aware that the sensual pleasure excited by music is not easy to retain within proper limits. The juridical code of the *Motu Proprio* spells out the safeguards and, in doing so, sets up a consistent system of aesthetic values. They are logically developed from the tenet that the music must always remain the humble handmaid of the text. Mozart used the same metaphor for the opposite purpose when writing that "in an opera, the poetry must be the handmaid of music." The autonomous musician will sympathize with Mozart's approach while recognizing, more or less reluctantly, the possibility of an inversion of the dogma. In order to be subservient to the purpose of the liturgy, church music must accordingly possess three qualities: it must be holy, true art, and universal. These terms might be difficult to define—for scholars and laymen alike. The Roman Catholic Church circumscribes them with a reference to Gregorian chant, which embraces the three desired qualities in the highest degree. A single unaccompanied melody will not obliterate the text; a free rhythm unshackled by strict meter wards off the association with unholy dance characteristics. The authority of St. Gregory and the testimonial of history vouch for the artistic goodness of the Gregorian melodies. Out of these two qualities of holiness and goodness, the third quality, universality, will spontaneously arise.

This axiomatic acceptance of Gregorian chant as a model reduces the aesthetics of church music to a single rule: "The more closely a composition for church approaches the Gregorian melody in movement, inspiration, and flavor, the more sacred and liturgical it is; and the more it departs from that supreme model, the less worthy it is of the temple."

Because the works of the sixteenth-century Roman composers, foremost among them Pierluigi da Palestrina, also possess in an eminent degree the qualities of holiness, goodness, and universality, and thereby come quite close to the supreme model of Gregorian chant, they deserve to be heard in the most solemn functions of the church service. The farthest possible departure from the model, on the other hand, is Italian opera music of the nineteenth century; hence it is least compatible with sacred music. Anything reminiscent of the conventionalism of the theatrical style, be it the rhythm or merely the external pattern of a profane piece, is therefore to be excluded from the church service. Into this category, and hence lacking the desired qualities, fall devices like repetition of words, breaking of syllables, concerto virtuosity, and individualistic expression. A chorus, being human yet impersonal, is the preferred instrument. It should be hidden behind gratings or at least behind ecclesiastical garb; and women, barred from holding a real liturgical function, cannot be admitted among the singers. The organ may support, but never oppress, the voices. A piano is strictly forbidden, and so are "noisy and frivolous instruments" such as percussion instruments. Bands, too, are profane, except outdoors or "with proper safeguards" determined by special permission. As a reminder of its secondary role to the liturgy, the music must be sufficiently short so as never to keep the priest at the altar waiting longer than is fitting to the ceremony.

With these guiding principles in mind (which condemn on many counts the Masses of Bach, Beethoven, Mozart, and Haydn), the visitor should attend services in the churches in Rome, preferably on Sunday mornings and holidays. The more the music he hears reminds him of *Tosca* rather than of plainchant, the less the particular service is in line with the sacred prescriptions of the *Motu Proprio;* but even if it sounds like dull secondhand Palestrina, there is no guarantee of its inherent goodness of form.

A tourist, by definition, is interested in places. The musical tourist will find singular satisfaction in the church of Santa Maria in Vallicella (on the Corso Vittorio Emanuele, nearer to the bridge than to the Capitoline Hill), where a particular room has given the name to an entire and popular type of musical composition. The prayer room, or *oratorio,* was originally part of the church, but it is now municipal property and accessible through a separate door to the left of the main entrance. The pleasant hall accommodates concerts and conferences. Here Filippo Neri, in the last decades of the sixteenth century when the church was new, assembled around him persons of all ages and social levels for common prayer meetings. Usually on Sunday nights, the ever-growing crowd listened to a short sermon, recited prayers, and embellished them with songs. In a way, these exercises translated a social situation into a spiritual experience. The sermon soon turned into the telling of a religious story, the recitation into a dialogue, and the simple music into a dramatic and exalted commentary on the Biblical incident. The enormous popularity of the Congregazione dei Preti dell'Oratorio gives one confidence that the sainthood bestowed on Filippo Neri within a generation after his death was merited by the salvation of many souls. The lasting popularity of the oratorio as a musical art form might permit even a heathen hearing Handel's *Messiah* or Haydn's *Creation* to think kindly of St. Philip as the originator. Less artistic souvenirs of the Saint, as well as various effigies, will be shown by the sacristan of Santa Maria in Vallicella; and the altar in the chapel left of the apse covers his earthly remains.

The musical contributors to the *oratorio* congregation

were first anonymous improvisers, but Palestrina himself was drawn into Neri's circle. The activities of this illustrious composer are described in the chapter of this book devoted to his birthplace, after which he is named. While considering the Roman churches, the visitor should only be reminded that Palestrina's music and person were a live part of the Sistine Chapel, San Giovanni in Laterano, Santa Maria Maggiore, and St. Peter's.

Fourteen years after Palestrina's death, when his pupil Francesco Soriano directed the Capella Giulia (as the choral forces of St. Peter's are called), the organist was suddenly dismissed *iustis de causis* and a twenty-five-year-old youngster from Ferrara was elected over heavy competition. (The narrow loser, Constantini, waited thirty-five years for the winner's death before he, at last, acceded to the organ.) Girolamo Frescobaldi—the visitor to Ferrara will remember—had imbibed a solid musical tradition, and his contribution to the music of Rome is second to none. One may readily believe the judgments of his contemporaries who see in him the *mostro degli organisti* ("the prodigy among organists"), the *stupore del tasto* ("the keyboard wonder"), or simply *ce grand Frescobaldi*. He was eminent as a composer and as an improviser. His stylistic inventions were daring, and soon no composer was esteemed unless he wrote in Frescobaldi's style. It is reported that thirty thousand listeners thronged St. Peter's Cathedral to hear his first performance on All Saints' Day 1608. The poorer among them may have begun to admire him the previous year during his short tour of service in Santa Maria in Trastevere (where not the smallest physical reminder of him is visible today).

Of the organs Frescobaldi played in Rome, one is still standing above the northern portal of the transept in San Giovanni in Laterano. This was not Frescobaldi's church, but the instrument was the best in town and suited his artistic aspirations. It was new then, having been installed by Luca Blasi, of Perugia, in 1597. Since the Second World War the organ has not been playable, but the original gilded case is as fabulous a sight as ever. In the front rank one discerns among the old Blasi pipes some that were baroquely twisted for ornamental reasons. The largest twenty-four-foot subcontra-*F* has a diameter of fifteen inches. The church of San Giovanni in Laterano has a special claim on organs, anyway. Pope Sylvester II (also known as Gerbert), who is buried in the church, not only translated Latin philosophers and constructed elaborate globes of astronomical spheres, but also built organs around the year 1000—activities that doubtless contributed to his reputation as an accomplished scholar during his lifetime and as a diabolic magician soon after his death.

Apparently the game of musical chairs was known to Italy of the Baroque. When Monteverdi had left Mantua for Venice in 1613, Cardinal Gonzaga, the Duke of Mantua, tried to lure Frescobaldi to his city. The composer demanded tenure and exorbitant sums of money. He traveled to the Gonzaga court but carefully left his family in Rome so that he easily returned when his conditions were met only in words but not in reality. After twenty years in Rome, he joined for a time the establishment of the Grand Duke of Tuscany, Ferdinand II de' Medici, who had heard him on a visit to Rome. Of Frescobaldi's years in Florence, we know less than of the warm welcome Rome gave him when he returned after an absence of six years. He played again at St. Peter's; he taught students from all over Europe; and he occupied comfortable quarters right behind Trajan's column (in a house corresponding today to the Via Magnanapoli No. 11, the northern façade of the Palazzo Roccagiovine). When he died at the age of sixty, the principal musicians of the city sang the Requiem Mass in the neighborhood church de' Santi Apostoli, where he was buried. The music lover on his way from the Piazza Venezia to the

Trevi Fountain will notice a memorial tablet in the right corner of the outside portico; the grave of Frescobaldi disappeared in the inundation of 1691.

One other tomb might be mentioned because of its signal location. Arcangelo Corelli had found a fertile soil in Rome for developing the Baroque forms of violin music that he had learned in Bologna. With the new style of his sonatas and *concerti grossi,* he impressed the splendid circle that gathered in the Palazzo Riario (now Corsini) in Trastevere around Queen Christina of Sweden, who had become a Roman Catholic after her abdication. The abundance of string players assembled by Cardinal Ottoboni on Monday nights in the Palazzo della Cancelleria emphasized the contrast between the concertizing virtuosi and the *grosso* accompaniment that Corelli cultivated. Here he once directed, as first violin, a Handel overture in the presence of the composer who, demanding a more impetuous and accentuated performance, snatched the violin from his hands to demonstrate his own style of playing. Corelli's reaction has been often quoted (he was Handel's senior by thirty-two years): "Ma, caro Sassone, questa musica è nello stile francese, di cui io non m'intendo!" ("But, my dear Saxon, this music is in the French style about which I know little!"). When Corelli died in 1713, his ecclesiastical patron buried him in the Pantheon; but the admission of a musician to this sanctuary had to be secured by a special Papal dispensation. (It was only much later that Antonio Canova had the idea of using the Pantheon for a national shrine by assembling in the rotunda the busts of famous Italians of all times and all trades.) Corelli's tomb in the Capella San Giuseppe, the first to the left of the entrance, notes the indulgence of Pope Clement XI together with the composer's excellent qualities of mind and incomparable skill in musical rhythms.

The foreign visitor will feel less like an outsider if he realizes that others like him have become part of Roman history. On the cool Monte Pincio, the Villa Medici, once the prison of Galileo Galilei, now houses the winners of the Grand Prix de Rome. This award was established in 1803 by the Institut de France. The Académie des Beaux-Arts in Paris, a branch of the Institut, permits the prize-winning candidates to live for several years at the Villa Medici, all expenses paid, in a manner distinguished primarily by its elegant style from comparable modern American awards. The luxurious life at the Villa Medici, which was designed with the assistance of Michelangelo for the Medici Pope Leo XI, may offer a partial explanation for the general insignificance of the contributions by the prize-winning composers over the last 160 years. But at least three of the musicians continued their growth both in Rome and after returning to France. Berlioz, Bizet, and Debussy all lived as pensioners in the Villa Medici, separated one from the other by approximately a quarter of a century. Because their experiences span most of the musical life of the nineteenth century in Rome, they are worth recalling, particularly as they were articulately described by each composer in turn.

Life at the Villa Medici, which may be inspected by visitors during a few limited hours each week, emerges plastically in the reactions of the three composers, who differed in background and temperament. Unlike Bizet and Debussy, Berlioz arrived in Rome rather mature. In 1831 he was already twenty-eight years old and the *Symphonie Fantastique* lay behind him. He had few illusions about the place: "The director's apartments are sumptuous, and an ambassador might envy them; but the pupils' rooms, with the exception of two or three, are small, inconvenient, and very badly furnished. . . . The library contains a fair collection of classical works, but absolutely no modern books. It is open to the students till three, and it is a great resource for those who have nothing to do; for it is only fair to say that they enjoy the most complete liberty, and, beyond sending a picture, drawing, engraving, or piece of music once a year to the Académie at Paris, nothing is required of them; they may work as much or as little as they choose." They greeted his arrival "with deafening shouts" and such horseplay that he had to "recover from the shock of the reception." But Berlioz "was soon quite at home in the daily routine . . . Our meals were heralded by a bell . . . and we all rushed in just as we were, without collars, in straw hats, blouses torn or smeared with clay, slippers—in fact, in our studio undress. . . . After dinner we generally wasted an hour or two in the gardens . . ." Occasionally, however, the students gathered in the moonlight around a little fountain and, accompanied by Berlioz' "paltry guitar," sang excerpts from Weber's operas and whole acts from Gluck's and Mozart's; "for," Berlioz admits, "in justice to my contemporaries at the Académie . . . their taste in music was anything but vulgar." Later in the evening the students used to flock to the Antico Caffè Greco, where Berlioz struck up a friendship with the young Glinka. Nothing need prevent the modern traveler from drinking an espresso at the same address below the Spanish stairs, Via dei Condotti No. 86.

Bizet in 1858 was barely twenty and very happy about his eye-opening trip, even about small bothersome details that are shared by the modern traveler: "My trunk was in Rome before me. Everything arrived in good condition, my clothes are not even wrinkled. My companions fared less well. Sellier had paint bottles in his trunk; all broke. Fortunately only his laundry was sullied. Heim's suits were full of creases. . . . It is true that I was asked to pay seventy-five francs for the delivery, but I am sending you the bill of lading and the receipt so that you may claim a refund. . . . And now a bit about our arrival in the Académie. We were given a grand reception by our colleagues who felt obliged to play delightful tricks on us: short-sheeted beds; broken and propped-up night tables which caused a terrible noise each time one touched them; etc. . . . I have the good fortune to sit at dinner between the nicest boys of the Académie. . . . I live in a precious Turkish room . . . with a marvelous view of Rome . . . The food is simple and excellent . . . Only the servants are sloppy; therefore I shall soon brush my clothes a bit." Bizet, too, made his fellow pensioners sing portions of Mozart's operas; but after giving music lessons to a painter and a sculptor, he confessed that he was "too much of an egotist to be a good teacher."

Between the arrivals at the Villa Medici of Berlioz and Bizet, twenty-seven years had elapsed; and exactly that many years after Bizet, in 1885, the twenty-two-year-old Debussy joined the art students on the Monte Pincio. He was rebellious and morose from the beginning. At the very moment he won the Prix de Rome, he lost, he tells us, all joy in it: "I saw clearly the worries and annoyances that the smallest official position brings in its train. Besides, I felt that I was no longer free." Some of his former companions gave him a friendly welcome in Rome, but he complained about them: "There is none of the warm friendship of the Paris days. They are stiff, and seem to be full of their own importance—there is too much Prix de Rome about these people." The life at the Villa Medici was to him a combination of "a cosmopolitan hotel, a private college, and a compulsory civilian barracks." He called his room "the Etruscan tomb" and noted that "its walls were painted green, and seemed to recede as one walked towards them." The director "never took the least interest in the students, except as regards administrative matters." If Debussy's fellow laureates nicknamed him "the Prince of Darkness," they merely took cognizance of his antipathy toward "the abominable villa," his criticism of "the artistic environment and the good comradeship that the older men talk about," and his resentment of "the life of a noncommissioned officer on full pay." The painter Hébert, with whom Debussy played violin sonatas by Mozart, detested Wagner; and Debussy studied *Tristan und Isolde* in solitude and with a passion that made him "forget the most elementary principles of politeness." He was still rude and rancorous at the centenary celebration of the Académie in 1903, when he reported: "One could have wished that in honor of the occasion some improvements had been made in the meals supplied to the Prix de Rome students . . . of the present day. We narrowly escaped poisoning, and dyspepsia is not a necessary addition to the aesthetic equipment of an artist."

If Berlioz, Bizet, and Debussy reacted to the Villa Medici in divers ways, they were unanimous about the level of the musical life in Rome. Each one of them, at three different periods of the nineteenth century, found it deplorable, and the reader will have to decide for himself whether their reports reflect the facts of the situation or the perennial and deep-rooted rift between French and Italian tastes in musical matters.

Berlioz rushed off to St. Peter's immediately after his arrival, but his "beautiful musical dreams were dispelled by the grim and hopeless reality . . . While the other arts are flourishing in all their vividness . . . glowing with the splendor of genius . . ., music alone is degraded to the level of a poor hunted slave, singing wretched verses with a threadbare voice . . ." He found the organ in St. Peter's "wretched," and the choir "producing no effect and in fact wholly inaudible in the largest church in the world." Attending High Mass on an especially festive occasion, Berlioz witnessed "an incredible state of degradation." The performers tuned their instruments "as noisily as if they had been in a theater" but played badly out of tune nevertheless. "The music was worthy of the performers. Regular cavatinas, each with its crescendo, cabaletta, organ points, and roulades; the whole an indescribable monster . . . and, to crown all, the solos in this strange farrago were sung in a soprano voice, proceeding from a big man with a rubicund face and an immense pair of black whiskers." Nor did Berlioz find the music in the theaters any better. The opera orchestra, "about as imposing and formidable as the Prince of Monaco's army, has all the qualities which are generally regarded as defects. . . . The words 'symphony' and 'overture' are used in Rome to designate a certain noise which the orchestra makes before the curtain rises, and to which no one ever listens. The names of Beethoven and Weber are scarcely known there. A learned abbé, belonging to the Sistine Chapel, told Mendelssohn that he heard someone speak of a young man of great promise called Mozart." (Mozart would have been close to eighty had he lived to hear this remark.) The only music Berlioz liked in Rome was of a totally different order, and the Christmas visitor to Rome can even today hear the *pifferari* or *zampognari* who come down from the Calabria mountains with bagpipes and other reed instruments, their legs wrapped in goatskins, to perform music before sacred shrines. They are still as picturesque as when Berlioz "spent hours watching them in the streets . . . They generally wear large brown cloth cloaks and pointed brigand hats, and there is a strange, wild air about them which is quite unique." Berlioz called their music "refreshing" and "impressive," and we cannot disagree.

Bizet, who had wholeheartedly accepted the life at the Académie and in Rome, was convinced "that there are no pianists in Italy and that one takes for a great artist anyone who can merely play the C-major scale with both hands." The condition of church music had obviously not changed since the days of Berlioz, for Bizet wrote to his mother: "The beautiful religious holidays are musically nothing but unworthy farces. The same three *Miserere* are sung forever. It will remain this way." Bizet resented having to dress up early in the morning and to wait four hours for admission to the Sistine Chapel, "all this to hear unbearable music . . . Inspiration is here only in the works of the masters and, more so, in those of God, in the meadows and the antiquities, but not in these ridiculous ceremonies." Even during Holy Week, he witnessed only "bad music and an unworthy comedy." Bizet loved Rome but not the city's musical activities. "There is much to admire here, but there are also many bad disappointments. Bad taste is poisoning Italy, a country that is being lost to art. Rossini, Mozart, Weber, Paer, Cimarosa are here unknown, disregarded, or forgotten. This is sad!" Verdi's success worried him, but he conceded that the Italian master, although lacking style, at least never bored him.

Debussy showed his low regard for the local musical scene by barely bothering to go out. At the Conservatoire in Paris he had neglected to attend César Franck's class in Gregorian chant, and now in Rome the music he heard in some churches charmed him mainly for its exoticism. The old church melodies doubtless influenced his later style. The opera house did not lure him, for he cared as little about the standard Italian repertoire as about the routine productions. But, like Berlioz, he was fascinated by an experience in popular music. The Neapolitan Polichinelle came to town. Debussy took great delight in the little orchestra, and particularly in the old bass-viol player, who accompanied the performances. He frequently attended the shows; and it is claimed that, more than the Roman operas, they left their mark on his musical vitality. Debussy's attitude toward his Roman life was so negative that he fled from the Villa Medici before completing his term, thereby forfeiting the privilege of an all-Debussy concert upon his return to Paris. The Académie des Beaux-Arts recognized that their prize-winning composer showed "a rather over-pronounced taste for the unusual," and hoped "that time and experience will bring salutary modifications to M. Debussy's ideas and compositions."

The day after his arrival at the Villa Medici, Berlioz was introduced by a common friend to Felix Mendelssohn, who was six years younger and immeasurably more famous and polished. Then twenty-two, Mendelssohn had already written the overture to *A Midsummer Night's Dream,* the "Reformation" Symphony, and many chamber-music works; he was beginning to sketch the "Scottish" and "Italian" symphonies; and he had conducted the epochal revival of Bach's *Passion According to St. Matthew.* The two youthful composers struck up a quick friendship which lasted a lifetime. Berlioz was sure that the only "endurable moments" of his first stay in Rome were due to Mendelssohn's presence; and years later, reminiscing about "dreaming together on the plains of Rome," they symbolically exchanged batons as Indians exchange tomahawks ("When the Great Spirit shall have sent us to hunt in the land of souls, may our warriors hang up our tomahawks together at the door of the council-chamber," Berlioz wrote to the "Chief Mendelssohn").

The friendship was genuine, but they quarreled over almost everything. The sophisticated German Jew and the unorthodox French *frondeur* made a strange pair. An episode described by Berlioz is typical: "One evening we were exploring the baths of Caracalla, and debating the question of the merits or demerits of human actions and of their reward in this life. Just as I had replied by some enormity—I forget what—to his religious and orthodox enunciations, his foot slipped and he rolled violently down a steep ruined staircase. 'Admire the divine justice,' said I, as I helped him up; 'I blaspheme, and it is you who fall.' " Berlioz considered Mendelssohn "a regular porcupine as soon as anyone began to talk about music," but he admired his junior's "marvellous power of rendering the most complicated score on the piano." Mendelssohn had rented quarters on the Piazza di Spagna No. 5 (no tablet marks the spot), a short walk from the Villa Medici. The sun shone all day long through two front windows on a good Viennese grand piano, and the landlord was a former captain in the French army. Whenever Berlioz felt overpowered by the sirocco, he found cheer in visiting Mendelssohn in his apartment and interrupting his indefatigable production. Far from minding, the younger friend would soothe Berlioz's spleen by playing for him now a Gluck aria on whose beauty they agreed, now the finished sketch of *Fingal's Cave;* and Berlioz, "lying peevishly on the sofa," hummed along.

But Mendelssohn was not blind to their incongruities. Shortly after their first encounter, he reported to his parents: "Berlioz is a caricature, without a spark of talent, fumbling about in the darkness and imagining himself to be the creator of a new world; he writes the most horrible things, and dreams and thinks of nothing but Beethoven, Schiller, and Goethe. In addition he is inordinately vain . . . I really cannot stand this assumption of genius; and if he were not a Frenchman, with whom it is always agreeable to associate and who are always interesting, I could not endure him any longer."

Mendelssohn belongs to a legion of people who are exhilarated and stimulated by Rome but disappointed and appalled by the musical experiences offered by the city. He was very explicit in his letters to his family and to his music teacher Carl Friedrich Zelter, Goethe's friend. If he had heard much about a special style and tradition of singing in the Papal Chapel, he was "able to detect very little of it." What he noticed was that the chorus often dropped in pitch; and that the leading tenor, whose music he once had an opportunity to see, was guilty of reading errors and uncertain attacks. The habit of freely embellishing a composition with ornaments produced to Mendelssohn's ears a most disagreeable effect; and what might under certain circumstances be considered a symptom of impromptu vitality, in the Sistine Chapel conveyed a lack of respect for the intentions of the composition.

Mendelssohn had anticipated much amusement at least from a premiere at a theater in Rome, but he "came away considerably out of humor." The music for that festive occasion was "so wretched that it is really beneath all criticism." The orchestras in Rome, too, "are worse than anyone could believe; both musicians, and the right feeling for music, are wanting. The violinists . . . make their entrances as and when they please; the wind instruments are tuned either too high or too low; and they execute flourishes like those we are accustomed to hear in farmyards, but hardly as good." Still, he did not care "that the wretched bassoonist squeaks in the orchestra," for everything becomes extraordinary in Rome. The Papal Choir does not sing particularly well, the compositions are poor, and the congregation is not devout, "and yet the whole effect was heavenly . . . It is the same as with everything else in this place; they may do as they like, build the most execrable houses, plant gardens in the worst taste, perform mediocre music; nature and the past are so rich that everything becomes beautiful and admirable."

We cannot leave nineteenth-century Rome without retracing some of the steps of Franz Liszt, whose character fitted that of the city peculiarly well. Here he could satisfy both his social and his religious cravings; he could mix with society and withdraw for introspective contemplation. He first visited Rome in 1839, when he was twenty-eight years old and already at a personal and artistic peak. His first reaction was typical of both an effusive traveler and a composer of program music: "Raphael and Michelangelo make Mozart and Beethoven more easy for me to understand . . . Titian and Rossini seem to me like stars of the same magnitude. The Colosseum and the Campo Santo are no longer strange," he writes to Berlioz, "if one thinks of your Heroic Symphony and your Requiem."

In 1861, Rome became Liszt's domicile, uninterruptedly so for the next eight years and shared with Weimar and Budapest until the end of his life two and a half decades later. The Princess Carolyne von Sayn-Wittgenstein had been his friend and companion for many years. She traveled to Rome in order to secure from the highest authority the consent for a divorce so that she might be free to marry Liszt. On the Via del Babuino No. 89, she occupied the third floor in winter and the fourth in summer, surrounded by fourteen busts of her lover. The house had belonged to the renowned Roman architect and city planner Giuseppe Valadier, and it had been honored in 1779—so a plaque inside the doorway tells us—by a personal visit of Pope Pius VI to Valadier's father. Here Liszt joined the Princess von Sayn-Wittgenstein two days before his fiftieth birthday, which they had selected to be their wedding day. The church of San Carlo al Corso was already decorated with flowers when a twelfth-hour message from the Vatican, far from annulling her early union to Prince von Sayn-Wittgenstein, forbade her to marry Liszt. They continued to see other daily, but he moved to separate quarters in the vicinity, at Via Felice (now Via Sistina) No. 113.

In those last years of the independent Papal State, Liszt decided to become a cleric—hardly because of his frustrated marriage plans (for he did not marry the Princess when she became a widow a few years later) but rather from a genuine desire for a peaceful retreat and also in the hope of becoming music director of the Vatican. His spiritual sponsor, Monsignor, later Cardinal, Hohenlohe, consecrated him in St. Peter's on 25 April 1865 and immediately assigned him an apartment in the Vatican, opposite the Logge of Raphael. There he smoked cigars with his friends, and from there he wrote to the Princess Carolyne: "Après demain votre très petit et infirme Abbé vous arrive avant 1 h." Two weeks later the German historian of Rome, Ferdinand Gregorovius, reported: "Yesterday I saw Liszt clad as an abbé—he was getting out of a hackney carriage; his black silk cassock fluttered ironically behind him—Mephistopheles disguised as an abbé. Such is the end of Lovelace."

Are there more splendid quarters in Rome than near the Logge of Raphael? The Villa d'Este in Tivoli was at the disposal of Monsignor Hohenlohe, who represented at the Vatican the interests of the Habsburgs, the legitimate owners at that time. The prelate furnished a suite for his friend Liszt; and the Villa d'Este remained the composer's home, his "El Dorado," in which he composed easily and productively. He had to make his own music up on the isolated hill; but at Christmas the *pifferari,* who had stimulated Berlioz' fancy, played their pipes before his house altar, and some of their tunes made their way into his scores. His pious exercises and devotional retreats did not help him make a musical career in the Vatican. His only Church promotion came many years later; and the Canon of Albano is still remembered today by a special Mass sung in the cathedral of that Roman hill town every 2 April, and paid for in perpetuity by a fund set up from his royalties. The journey from the Villa d'Este to the Piazza di Spagna took four hours in a public carriage, and Liszt was relieved when a new tramway eventually shortened the twenty-mile ride. It took sixty hours from Rome to Budapest. Liszt's *vie trifurquée* might be easy in an age of jet planes, but we must imagine him year after year in an oil-lit railroad compartment, often sitting up all night in a second-class carriage when he was either unwilling or unable to match the luxury of his trips with that of his Roman quarters.

In 1876 Carolyne von Sayn-Wittgenstein was still living at Via del Babuino No. 89, smoking cigars and writing an extravagant specialized history of the Roman Catholic Church, when Richard Wagner with his wife Cosima Liszt checked in at the Albergo d'America, a few doors down at No. 79. He was exhausted after the first Bayreuth festival and needed an Italian vacation. One can get a whiff of the former splendor and magnitude of the hotel (now converted into apartments and offices) by looking at the carriage entrance around the back at Via Margutta No. 67, where the name of the former Albergo d'America is still faintly visible in the old paint. Wagner stayed nearly a month, during which he met Gobineau for the first time. None of his operas had yet been heard in the city.

The spirit of Rome has apparently not provided the best climate for musical theaters. The Teatro dell'Opera was started in the late nineteenth century as a commercial venture, and the performances continue to sound commercial—less exacting than at the Teatro alla Scala in Milan and less elegant than at the Teatro di San Carlo in Naples. Typically enough, the earliest noteworthy premiere in the building was the result of a cash competition for a one-act opera, Mascagni's *Cavalleria Rusticana* in 1890 (which enabled the composer to spend most of his life at an elegant address, Via del Corso No. 122–124). Puccini's *Tosca,* ten years later, stands out as the only other estimable new venture. The builder of the theater, Domenico Costanzi, was a real-estate speculator who was also responsible for the Hotel Quirinale, near the opera house. A plaque visible from the Via Nazionale establishes the connection between Costanzi's two enterprises by reminding the passerby that Verdi appeared at the window of his hotel suite in April 1893 to greet a midnight crowd of several thousand on the occasion of Falstaff's entry into Rome. A less ostentatious memorial to the same incident is a stone slab, originally fastened to a toolshed in the old railroad station and now located in the Museo di Roma in the Palazzo Braschi (on the Corso Vittorio Emanuele): "In this room Giuseppe Verdi took shelter from the impetuous enthusiasm of the applauding crowd on his arrival in Rome on 13 April 1893."

There are two other opera houses in the city, however, which are older in years, richer in memories, and more intimate in appearance than Costanzi's building. The Teatro Valle, near the Piazza Navona, dates back to 1727. Rossini's *La Cenerentola,* which has recently gained new popularity, was first heard in the Teatro Valle in 1817; and so were, in subsequent years, several minor operas by Donizetti. Actors eventually replaced the singers. The music lover will not mind knowing that Eleonora Duse, Rachel, and Sarah Bernhardt appeared on the stage where now he hears only an occasional *stagione* of opera. If some leftover snowflakes of one night's *La Bohème* descend on the Sicilian heat of next night's *Cavalleria Rusticana,* the atmosphere of the old building becomes all the more special.

The Teatro Argentina, facing the Republican excavations that encroach upon the Corso Vittorio Emanuele, is presently used for concerts. Four years younger than the Teatro Valle, it owes its popularity to an opulence of style and a bit of notoriety to *The Barber of Seville.* One readily admires the willingness of a theater to produce a new work by a twenty-four-year-old composer, but the audience at the Teatro Argentina in 1816 booed the most sparkling of all Rossini operas, and only subsequent performances changed the original failure to success. In the 1840's, Verdi wrote two operas for the Teatro Argentina, *I due Foscari* and *La Battaglia di Legnano.* Neither one of them ever became popular.

Behind the building, on the Corso Vittorio Emanuele, stands the church of Sant'Andrea della Valle; and only a true opera fanatic will care to know that here, in an unidentifiable chapel, Cesare Angelotti found temporary refuge from the police forces of Baron Scarpia.

We are not frivolous to remind ourselves that fiddling while Rome burns is an old local custom.

ROVERETO

THE TRAVELER from the north approaching Italy by the traditional route across the Brenner Pass will reach Rovereto on his way from Trent to Verona. At the entrance to the town, the broad road is narrowed by a jutting stone house, now identified as Corso Bettini No. 7, and formerly as the Albergo della Rosa. A plaque records the fact that Goethe spent the night of 11 September 1786 in the hotel, and his diary reveals his delight at having to speak the beloved Italian language for the first time to the innkeeper and the postilion. Like all travelers, he must have changed horses in the establishment up the street, at No. 33, which reveals its old function and not merely by the sale of Esso gasoline.

The same route and the same hotel were used seventeen years earlier by Leopold and Wolfgang Mozart on their first Italian journey. They stayed four days at the "Rose." Now harboring office employees rather than weary travelers, the guest rooms are easily accessible and fundamentally unchanged. After ascending one flight of the original staircase, one finds in the corner apartment on the left behind eighteenth-century doors and brass locks the well-proportioned and airy rooms through the front windows of which Goethe, Mozart, and numerous other travelers looked out toward the Alps.

Wolfgang gave his first concert on Italian soil in the snug Baroque Todeschi Palace, Via Mercerie No. 14, which one can visit to the extent to which the modern apartment dwellers permit it. The day after Christmas 1769, the fourteen-year-old musician wanted to try out the organ in the principal church, San Marco. Although only a handful of people had been told that he was coming, accompanied by his father, all Rovereto seemed assembled there; and some robust fellows had to walk ahead and clear a way to the choir. Even then it took long minutes before Wolfgang could sit down at the organ, for everybody wished to get close to him. The organ looks today as it did then, but the sound has been modernized.

There was no commotion when Johannes Brahms visited Rovereto in 1884 on one of his Italian vacation trips. He did not like ostentation, anyway.

At Corso Bettini No. 70–78, near the Albergo della Rosa and across the street from the coach station, a lovely theater will please the visitor admitted by the custodian living in the building. Opened with a Cimarosa opera in 1784 (*Giannina e Bernardone,* which had been successfully running through Italy and some other European countries since 1781), it has been renamed after the gifted epigonal opera composer Riccardo Zandonai, who was born in a suburb of Rovereto in 1883. Of his nine operas, *Conchita* and *Francesca da Rimini* reached the Metropolitan Opera House in New York shortly before the United States entered the First World War; and they are still heard in Italy.

SIENA

THIS CITY, many visitors agree, is unlike any other city in Italy. They may mean the subtle dialect, the black-and-white architecture, or the giddying lines and lights; but they could as well mean the musical accomplishments of Siena, which are untypical in their significance and individualistic in their appearance. Actually, one finds neither preeminent composers nor momentous compositions in the rich history of Siena. But a few phenomena are noteworthy because they seem unique in their emphasis.

The visitor to the Palio, the race celebrated every 2 July and 16 August in the Piazza del Campo, should not be so distracted by the horses as to ignore the special silver trumpets. They are the products of a tradition older than that of the Palio. A company of *tubatores* and other wind players, i.e., a town band, is documented as early as 1040; and Sienese goldsmiths became famous all over Europe for the manufacture of precious trumpets.

From one public summer feast to the next, Siena society provided its own amusement. More than in other towns, it seems, the upper-class families were strongly addicted to various sophisticated and complex games, which were played in private homes in the evening and the artistic level of which adjusted itself to the capability of the participants, which was high. The reliance on one's own resources furnished just about the only form of entertainment after Siena lost its political independence in 1557 and public life became definitively subjugated by the old enemy Florence. Private clubs, or academies, were founded; and a recorded total of forty-six such organizations indicates the abundance of a particular style of social and artistic activity. The Accademia degli Intronati ("of the Stunned"), one of the oldest and most elegant clubs, mixed singing, dancing, and playing with intellectual contests, debates, and riddles. Some of the members published treatises on the merry and capricious games and on the music that went with them, indulged in by the graceful ladies and young men of Siena. The evening parties, or *veglie,* of the Intronati challenged the fantasy of many artists. One of the results was a singularly large, quaint, and celebrated composition by Orazio Vecchi, a contemporary of Shakespeare and choir director in the Modena Cathedral.

Vecchi called the piece *Le Veglie di Siena* and explained in a subtitle his intention to present the various humors expressible in music. *Le Veglie di Siena* is a collection of forty-seven choral pieces for three, four, five, and six voices. They are divided into two parts: a gay evening and a serious evening. Both are based on the time-honored principle that the arts imitate life; and in a learned preface the composer quotes Aristotle, Horace, and Castiglione. In the facetious part, Vecchi caricatures in music an uncultured Sicilian, a coquettish country girl, a German trying to speak Italian, a sentimental Spaniard, an amorous Frenchman, a supercilious Venetian, and a group of wailing Jews. (The treatment of the last is akin to that of Shylock, who is comical because outlandish; and it differs from that of Samuel Goldenberg and Schmuyle by Moussorgsky, which sounds anti-Semitic.) The second, grave, evening party warms up with a few games: love is hunted, and the six choral voices in turn make "tuh tuh" like horns and "bau bau" like dogs. Then a *bisticcio* is sung, a play on words of which the following line is merely a sample: "Prese la pazza le pizze e le pezze, e le gittò nel pozzo." But the tone soon turns serious, and one hears rich choruses imitating humors identified, among others, as *licenzioso, dolente, lusinghiero, malenconico, gentile, affettuoso, perfidioso,* and *balzano* ("licentious, grievous, flattering, melancholy, gentle, affectionate, perfidious, and capricious").

Orazio Vecchi's *Le Veglie di Siena* was printed in 1604. In the same decade a musician of ancient Sienese aristocracy was so happy and proud to be admitted to the membership of the Accademia degli Intronati that he began to sign his compositions "Academico armonico intronato." His name was Agostino Agazzari, and he should be remembered as the only Sienese composer of international importance. He died in 1640 as music director of the Siena Cathedral after his name had become associated with Antwerp, Salzburg, and Rome. He was a most versatile composer and theorist, quoted and translated north of the Alps for his authoritative treatment of the new expressive Baroque style, and the first to make literary use of the legend that Palestrina's *Missa Papae Marcelli* had saved Roman Catholic church music.

While Agazzari was making music in the Siena Cathedral, the beautifull *tarsia* choir stalls were already in place and the illuminated choir books were on their sculptured desks, as they are today, in the Piccolomini Library off the left aisle. He also must have occasionally stepped across the Piazza del Duomo into the hospital church of Santa Maria della Scala; and if he played the little organ suspended on the right wall, the sounds he heard were the same we can hear today. The instrument was built in 1518 by local masters—the musical part probably by Giovanni Piffaro, and the case by the architect Baldassare Peruzzi. Recent restorations have not altered the character of the six registers, among which the gentle diapasons and the sharp choir voices, all metal, gain specific liveliness from an uneven wind pressure. The elegance of the carved case is architectural rather than pictorial; the topmost figure looks as if conducting the musical *putti* and the organist below.

The Accademia degli Intronati was so close to the political heart of Siena that the former hall of the great council in the Palazzo Pubblico was converted into a theater in the sixteenth century and eventually turned over to an offspring of the Stunned, the Accademia dei Rinnovati. Today the parent Accademia degli Intronati occupies rather modest quarters in a municipalized palace at Via di Città No. 75–77 (near the Piazza del Campo). But the Teatro dei Rinnovati is the pride of the city. Originally built almost wholly of wood, it has been burned down twice. In its present appearance, freshened in 1950, it follows an eighteenth-century design by one of the Bibienas. Admission can be gained through the guarded door at the right rear of the left courtyard (diagonally across from the entrance to the tower).

Another club, the Accademia dei Rozzi ("of the Roughs") was the closest rival of the Intronati in age, status, imagination, and initiative. One can readily see how it has continued to flourish. The club property covers the area of a large block in the heart of town. The name "Accademia dei Rozzi" is proudly displayed over the entrance at Via di Città No. 34–36, where the vertex of this curved main street lies. The posted membership list reads like a genealogical register of Siena. The attractive clubrooms include a private concert hall and a direct corridor to the Teatro dei Rozzi, the public entrance to which, marked in gold letters, is around the corner on the Piazza Indipendenza. Even the custodian, living at the back at Via di Diacceto No. 17, has a direct passageway from his apartment to the auditorium. The Teatro dei Rozzi, opened in 1690, doubtless represents the style of an eighteenth-century theater at its best. Restoration is in progress to add modern safety to old charm.

Both these handsome theaters have been given a new lease

on life by the highly individualistic activities of a Sienese nobleman, Count Guido Chigi-Saracini. In his fourteenth-century palace, at the central Via di Città No. 89, he founded in 1932, in established local tradition, an Accademia Chigiana which has become famous for summer courses culminating in the Settimana Musicale, a musical week, each September. Under Count Chigi-Saracini's personal direction, master classes are held, chamber music is played, old operas are revived in lively performances, manuscript scores are reproduced in facsimile editions, and historical and scholarly essays are printed and discussed. The main front hall one flight up is characteristically given over to an intimate and elegant auditorium. The Palazzo Chigi-Saracini also houses an extensive picture gallery which is opened to the outsider who officially applies to the owner for admission. The Accademia Chigiana under the same roof concentrates in one focal point all the musical characteristics of Siena: centuries of tradition, private enterprise, and unusual results.

The taste of Siena must be untypical even in trivial matters.The singer Nicolini sang in an opera company in this city in August 1770 and was very much approved, but the same performers in the same compositions were totally disliked and neglected at Lucca in September.

SORRENTO

This is what a foreign traveler, sailing by the Sorrento peninsula long ago, had to say about the music he heard from the shore: "The breeze dropped, some power lulled the waves, and a breathless calm set in. . . . Lovely voices came to me across the water, and my heart was filled with a longing to listen . . . 'Draw near,' they sang, 'and bring your ship to rest so that you may hear our voices. No seaman ever sailed his ship past this spot without listening to the sweet tones that flow from our lips, and none that listened has not been delighted and gone on a wiser man.' "

The traveler was Odysseus, about three thousand years ago; the singers were the Sirens. There is nothing to prevent the modern tourist from falling under a similar spell if he trusts his ears.

STRA

THE ROAD FROM Padua to Venice, along the Brenta River, passes many villas of the ancient Venetian nobility. About eight miles from Padua is the little village of Stra with the wonderful seventeenth-century Villa Pisani. It can also be easily reached from Venice by boat, bus, or car (preferably by boat up the Brenta: regular public transportation and special excursion trips leave from the Riva degli Schiavoni). The villa will speak for itself, and the guide will point out the room in which Hitler and Mussolini held a conference. The visitor interested in a musical curio should pay attention to an unobtrusive eighteenth-century picture in a room facing the garden. Far from being great art, it shows the inside of a Venetian theater, the audience enjoying an all-girl orchestra, including two female bass-viol players, and an all-girl chorus. The conductor at the harpsichord, however, is a male. The painting probably represents a concert by one of the four reputable *ospedali* in Venice.

TRENT

THE NAME OF this city (which has an old but generally modest musical history) evokes in the musician two isolated but extraordinarily significant associations. One concerns a collection of manuscripts, the other a collection of men; and the impact of either on the status of our civilization cannot be overrated.

The Bishop of Trent in the second half of the fifteenth century, Johann Hinderbach, was one of the most learned men of his time. For his private library he had copied on well over two thousand sheets a wide selection of contemporary sacred and secular music. He drew not only on sources in Italy and Germany but also in England, France, and the Netherlands. A few of the compositions actually celebrate events that happened in the South Tyrol (Alto Adige) and in Trent. Gathered into seven volumes known as the Trent Codices, the 1,864 compositions form the richest source of our knowledge of fifteenth-century music. The names of Dunstable, Leonel, Ockeghem, Binchois, and Dufay crown a gigantic array of less explored but fascinating musical craftsmen.

Doubtless the property of the chapter of Trent Cathedral, the Codices were transcribed and partly published by the Austrian government; for Trent did not belong to Italy until the end of the First World War in 1918. At that time, the first six volumes, which had been sold to the Austrian Ministry of Education in 1891, were returned to Trent; they were enhanced by the discovery of a seventh volume in the archives in 1920; and today they may be called for in the Museo Nazionale Trentino in the Castello del Buon Consiglio by their identification numbers, Codices Tridentini 87–93. They are kept under lock in the same room in which a faïence stove normally invites admiration. Behind the original leather bindings, the first leaf appropriately sings a *Gloria,* as composed by Dufay.

The Bishop of Trent has earned our gratitude, but his catholic taste (if a pun be permitted) played into the hands of the Protestant reformation. Luther, who was active in the generation following the completion of the Trent Codices, opened the church doors to almost any kind of music. But his unreformed friend Erasmus worried about what he heard in places of worship: "We have introduced an artificial and theatrical music into the church, a bawling and agitation of various voices, such as I believe had never been heard in the theaters of the Greeks and Romans. Horns, trumpets, pipes vie and sound along constantly with the voices. Amorous and lascivious melodies are heard such as elsewhere accompany only the dances of courtesans and clowns. The people run into the churches as if they were theaters, for the sake of the sensuous charm of the ear."

It was in Trent that the Council convened—almost exactly one century after Bishop Hinderbach's reign—which planned to counteract the rising Protestant force. The city is full of reminders of the occasion—the crucifix in the Duomo, before which the decrees of the Council were promulgated; an illustrative canvas in the church of Santa Maria Maggiore, where several sessions were held; and the grandiose Castello del Buon Consiglio, which served as a headquarters. The Counter Reformation concerned itself with all aspects of the physical and spiritual life, and music occupied the attention of the Council during the last of its eighteen years. The visitor to Rome has acquainted himself with the modern attitude of the Roman Catholic Church toward music: the *Motu Proprio* of 1903 makes clear and positive recommendations. The rules laid down by the Council of Trent were prohibitory and outlined desirable results rather than musical means. At the twenty-second general session, on 17 September 1562, the Council approved a committee recommendation to ban from church music all lascivious or impure melodies, whether sung or played on the organ. Music must not give empty pleasure to the ear but draw the hearts of the listeners to the desire of heavenly harmonies.

These exhortations apparently sounded too vague to be effective. The whole question of music was reconsidered the following year (the last of the Council) at the request of some cardinals who associated any polyphonic music in the church with "scandalous noises." One of the strongest proponents of this attitude was the Bishop of Palestrina—an ironic fact if one remembers the legendary role of his contemporary compatriot as the "savior of music." Equally ironic is the emergence of Cardinal Carlo Borromeo as an advocate of polyphonic music; for in the ascetic spirit of the Counter Reformation, he had just stripped his own cathedral in Milan—even the gorgeous tombs of his relatives—of earthly ornaments and decorations. As a member of a special commission, he probably listened to entreaties by the Emperor Ferdinand I as much as to the various compositions by Kerle, Palestrina, Lasso, and others—all of which successfully made the point that contrapuntal art could be reconciled with ecclesiastical demands.

URBINO

THE DUCAL PALACE is the setting for the discussions held on four March evenings in 1507 on the characteristics of a perfect courtier. The participants—among them Pietro Bembo, Cesare Gonzaga, and Giuliano de' Medici—may appear idealized in the conversation as reported by Baldassare Castiglione; but *Il Cortegiano* has remained a classic of Renaissance prose—earning the title *Il Libro d'Oro* in Italy and being available in a modern paperback edition in America. Duke Guidobaldo Montefeltro of Urbino aspired to make his court the most refined and elevated in Italy. Castiglione, one of the many aristocratic artists and statesmen attracted by him, was as skillful in political missions (as, for instance, to Henry VII in England and Charles V in Spain) as in his poetry in Latin and Italian. The emperor called him "one of the world's best cavaliers," and the ideal gentleman of the Italian Renaissance emerges from the discussions in the *Cortegiano*.

What interests us here is that the ideal gentleman was expected to be musical, as the friends meeting in the ducal drawing room would agree. Music is not only an ornament but a necessity for a gentleman. Besides being the most honest and praiseworthy leisure activity, in which each man finds refreshment from daily vexations, it pleases the tender and soft breasts of women, who have always counted it a most acceptable food of the mind. When one of the discussion partners wonders whether music is a vanity fit for women but not for men, a host of masculine witnesses is conjured up from revived antiquity and culled from contemporary reality. "It has been the opinion of most wise philosophers that the world is made of music, and the heavens in their moving make a melody, and our soul framed after the very same sort, and therefore lifts up itself and (as it were) revives the virtues and force of it with music." Alexander the Great conquered mighty nations but succumbed to the influence of rousing and relaxing melodies. Socrates learned to play the lyre when he was advanced in age and wisdom. Plato and Aristotle advocated music instruction for every man to incline him toward virtue. The militant Spartans and the valiant Cretans used soft instruments; and the Athenian general Themistocles, who did not, was a great deal the worse for it. Even Achilles learned music from his master, the centaur Chiron; and if the hands that shed so much Trojan blood were often occupied in playing upon the lyre, what modern soldier should think it a shame to follow Achilles? God must have given music to man for a most sweet lightening of our travails and vexations. The laborer sings in the field, the peasant woman at the spinning wheel, the mariners on the rough seas, the pilgrims on weary voyages, the prisoners in jail; and "a man would judge that nature had taught it unto nurses for a special remedy to the continual wailings of sucking babes, which at the sound of their voices fall into a quiet and sweet sleep, forgetting the tears that are so proper to them, and given us of nature in that age for a guess of the rest of our life to come."

The kind of music best suited for a courtier is solo singing to the accompaniment of a stringed instrument, because thus all the sweetness of music is contained in one voice. One can follow the performance and the melody more attentively and clearly "when the ears are not busied in hearing any more than one voice." The Renaissance emphasis on the individual considers it almost a virtue that in a solo song every little error is soon perceived, unlike the situation in a chorus where one voice carries the other. The old Greeks had made a moral distinction between stringed and wind instruments. The *Cortegiano* echoes it by recommending the former as perfect and sweet while rejecting the latter as noisome. Gentility in music as in other matters is apparently a quality required of a gentleman. As a model, Castiglione sets up his friend Marchetto Cara, who had successfully composed one of his sonnets. Cara is praised for his soft harmonies, his placid style full of tearful gentleness, and his tender penetration of the soul with sweet and delightful emotions. But the seasoning of the whole practice of music must be discretion and good taste. A gentleman who is a righteous judge of himself will know when to make music and when not.

Raphael was born in Urbino; the portrait he painted of Baldassare Castiglione hangs in the Louvre in Paris. But with all its genuineness, Urbino was far less successful translating the concern for music into reality than, for instance, Mantua or Ferrara. Guidobaldo's father, Federigo, was one of the most glamorous rulers in the history of Urbino. His portrait by Piero della Francesca in the Uffizi in Florence, facing that of his wife Battista, attracts attention as much by the duke's strong features as by the allegorical triumphs on the reverse of the panels. Yet a manuscript preserved in the Vatican which lists Federigo's munificent establishment in detail accounts for only three singers and two organists in a household of 317 personal employees. The total of five musicians appears diminutive against the same number of readers during meals, or tapestry workers, or kitchen chefs—let alone against fourteen public clerks or nineteen table waiters. Three professional choristers cannot accomplish very much, even when occasionally supported by five singing boys and housed next to six military trumpeters and two drummers.

All the talking about music apparently did not produce

or attract any significant musicians. The name of Marco Antonio Cavazzoni comes to mind, a composer born in Urbino about the same time as Raphael. His collection of organ works, of which the only extant copy lies in the British Museum in London, is among the earliest and most original in all organ literature. But he left Urbino as a child and earned his laurels mostly in Venice in the circle around Willaert.

VENICE

THE BASILICA OF San Marco is the brilliant focal point of the whole city. Even the doges in their considerable political might respected this fact when erecting their palace within the immediate sphere of the basilica. The visual splendor of San Marco seems undiminished. The musical splendor once matched it. In the sixteenth century in particular, the position of choir director and first organist was the most coveted in musical Europe, and it was regularly filled by the best available musician of the generation. One must bear in mind that a Renaissance musician was a total musician, not a specialist like his modern counterpart. The choir director and organist composed the music he needed. Performer and composer were one. The musician's teaching responsibilities increased with his fame, and to the publication of his music was often added that of his theoretic treatises.

The political supremacy of Venice in Europe was mirrored by the musical supremacy of San Marco. Thus we have a long row of supreme masters setting the musical tone, from the fifteenth to the seventeenth centuries at least, of more than the church service in Venice. The tradition was continuous; for the *maestro di cappella* at the first organ would usually be followed by his pupil who had spent years under his tutelage at the second organ. The tourist who has enjoyed the canvases of Bellini, Carpaccio, and Titian should listen with comparable respect, pleasure, and admiration to the compositions of Jean

Mouton, Adrian Willaert, Cyprian de Rore, Zarlino, Andrea Gabrieli, his nephew Giovanni Gabrieli, and Monteverdi. The glamour and brilliant artistry of the Venetian style have lost none of their special sheen over the centuries, as a painting might under layers of dust and varnish. We concede that more initiative and effort may be required for bringing old music to life than for looking at an old painting in a museum. The task is facilitated by the recent flood of phonograph records, not to mention concerts of old music and amateur choirs in which one can participate in singing Willaert and Gabrieli.

The transition from Netherlandish to Italian names in the line of musicians typifies a general trend of sociological interest. Around 1500, the Netherlands was the undisputed musical center of Europe, exporting not only compositions but composers. Hence the preponderance of Flemish names among musicians in Italy. By 1600, the Italians had learned from their foreign masters all they could, and they established themselves in their homeland with deserved autonomy. By 1700, the abundance of Italian musicians had shifted the musical center of gravity to such an extent that Italian musicians flooded the rest of Europe.

When Venice was at its height, music students from all over flocked there as they do today to New York or Paris. Among them we single out the German Heinrich Schütz, who was born in 1585 exactly one century before Bach and Handel. He is one of the supreme musical masters of the seventeenth century in Germany and of all times. He studied in Venice from 1609 to 1613 with Giovanni Gabrieli, who had taken leave from the first organ at San Marco because of sickness during the last years of his life. Gabrieli gave Schütz his precious seal ring on his deathbed as if to confirm the passing on to him of his musical knowledge and craft. Schütz, whose compositions fill eighteen folio volumes, wrote the first German opera, *Dafne,* in 1627.

The musical vitality of San Marco in the late Renaissance gained strength from a long tradition of local organ players and organ builders. Venetians excelled in organ construction from the sixth century on and supplied organs and organists to the rest of Europe throughout the Middle Ages. The practice of supporting a church choir by the organ seems common to most of us today, even at a Roman Catholic service. But actually Venice must be greatly credited for withstanding the Roman pressure for unaccompanied, *a cappella,* singing. In upholding the grandeur of the organ, Venice was doubtless influenced by the Orient, with which a rich trade formed a cultural link and of which the style of St. Mark's Cathedral is not the only residue.

With the Byzantine style of the cathedral came the Byzantine habit of antiphonal singing, i.e., of pitching two distinct choruses against each other. No wonder that St. Mark's had become the seat of two organs by 1316, establishing a musical style that is as characteristic of Venice as the pictorial style of the Bellinis. The architecture of the cathedral favors the arrangement. From the top of the campanile one easily sees the four cupolas surrounding in cross-form a more prominent fifth in the center. The roundness of the halls below these five cupolas, visually and acoustically quite dissimilar from the elongated nave of a Gothic cathedral, creates an awesome resonance. The two organs, with the adjoining choir lofts, are up on a gallery to the right and left of the altar. Arches open on several sides into the center of the basilica. The sound flowing through them hits the ears of the congregation gathered under the central cupola from both sides, like the right and left punches of a boxer. What a glamorous conception of music! Not to be found anymore today, for the organs have been inadequately remodeled. They no longer match each other, and the music staff of San Marco, it seems, has its hands full with one organ and one choir. The winged doors of the south organ, painted by Gentile Bellini in 1464, are in the cathedral museum. Perhaps the current revival of Renaissance and Baroque music will help restore the double-choir and double-organ practice of San Marco, to the benefit of future musicians and churchgoers.

No doubt, the healthy musical life of Venice during the Renaissance had much to do with the appearance and establishment there of the first music printing done anywhere. To touch and see some concrete evidence, the traveler can do no better than visit the Biblioteca Nazionale Marciana, founded in 1468 and now installed in Sansovino's old palace of the Zecca (Mint) across from the Doge's Palace on the Piazzetta. The entrance to the library is at No. 7 beneath the arcade (and behind some coffeehouse tables). A guard in the hallway will issue library call slips upon request. The visitor interested in a rare musical experience should fill out three to begin with: MUS 197–198–199, *Motetti;* MUS 200–201–202, *Motetti;* and MUS 209–210–211, *Missarum Liber*. After handing the slips to the attendant in the large reading room at the right rear of the hallway, the visitor will have to wait only a short time before holding in his hands some of the earliest, most valuable, and most beautiful printing of music that has ever been done.

Ottaviano Petrucci is credited with being the first printer of music from movable type, but it is the exquisite quality of his workmanship and his superior musical and visual taste that vie for our attention with mere priority. Gutenberg had printed his first Bible in 1454. Fifteen years later, two Germans from Speyer imported printing to Venice, then one of the cultural capitals of the Western world. On 25 May 1498, Petrucci, thirty-two years old, obtained from the Signoria in Venice an exclusive privilege, a monopoly for twenty years, to print and publish music in the Venetian Republic. The legal statement can be seen on the last page of MUS 199, the bass part of the motets, next to the memorable Petrucci imprint: " . . . quod nullus possit cantum Figuratum imprimere sub pena . . ." (". . . nobody else may print music, under penalty . . .").

The first music ever printed appeared in 1501, a collection of about one hundred of the best compositions of the time. According to the practice of the day, the compositions were not printed in score, i.e., the parts one above the other on one page, but in separate part-books, so that every singer had only his own part in front of him. This explains the several volumes in each set now in the hands of the traveler, all of which appeared in the first decade of the century. MUS 197–198–199 contain the soprano, alto, and bass parts of a collection of motets by such leading composers as Josquin Des Prez, Mouton, and Agricola. The set is incomplete (though the missing parts can be found elsewhere). A vista at backstage politics is opened up by the stamp on these volumes of the Vienna National Library: "Bibliotheca Palat. Vindobonensis." These Petrucci prints have served as war trophies, moving from Venice to Vienna and back, depending on which of the two powers in their various struggles during the last centuries happened to hold the upper hand. MUS 200–201–202, also a collection of superb motets, testify to Petrucci's handsome layout and supreme legibility, although the paper has yellowed more than that of the other set. The Masses, finally (MUS 209–210–211), among which the great Obrecht and Brumel are represented, are resplendent in their whiteness and display of proportion.

The church was the one place throughout the Middle Ages where the general population could hear good music. Public theaters began to appropriate this particular function of the church in the late Renaissance—in Venice more quickly than elsewhere. The musicians of San Marco had made their contribution to the musical heritage of the whole world before the organ was pushed into the background in the seventeenth and eighteenth centuries by the new craze for musical theater. This dichotomy prompted an eighteenth-century visitor, Baron Pöllwitz, to say of the Venetians that "they spend one half of their time in committing Sin, and the other half in begging God's Pardon."

The transition from church to theater, from psalm to opera, is dramatized by Monteverdi's life. Having gained fame in Mantua, he was invited to try out for the most desirable music position of the time, that of *maestro di cappella* at St. Mark's in Venice, by giving a recital there on 19 August 1613. His appointment was unanimous, his salary relatively high, and the position was his until he died thirty years later. He lived in the *canonica,* the quarters reserved for the clerical staff, accessible then as now directly from the left side of the choir (before the sacristy) or from the Calle de Canonica, which runs along the left side of the cathedral. The *canonica* was fully remodeled in 1953 when the future Pope John XXIII settled in it as Patriarch of Venice; but the atmosphere of the inner courtyard, the *corte de canonica,* cannot have changed much over the centuries. In the cathedral, Monteverdi directed thirty singers and more than twenty instrumentalists, an occupation which kept him at first from following up the success of his early operas in Mantua. "Considera che il mio servitio ecclesiastico m'haveva un poco slontanato dal genere di teatro," he wrote to his old friend and librettist Striggio. His church service removed him at first from writing for the theater. He even was consecrated as a priest and called "Reverendo" on the title page of a 1632 publication.

In 1637, when Monteverdi was entering his seventh decade, the first public opera house anywhere was opened in Venice in the parish of San Cassiano with a performance of *Andromeda* by Francesco Manelli (whose participation in the opening is his major claim to musical fame). By the end of the century, sixteen new theaters in Venice had produced a total of 358 different operas.

One year after the San Cassiano, the Teatro San Moisè opened with Monteverdi's old *L'Arianna,* but in the next four years he wrote four new operas. *Il Ritorno d'Ulisse in Patria* in 1640 and *L'Incoronazione di Poppea* in 1642, the latter for the Teatro San Giovanni e Paolo, have survived and are still performed today. They attest to the extraordinary vitality of the aging composer, who had completely mastered the new trend and made it his own, undaunted by a long and painful widowerhood, the capture of his doctor son in Bologna by the Inquisition, and sixteen months of the plague in Venice. The city mourned his death in 1643 by Solemn Requiem Masses in the two principal churches of San Marco and Santa Maria Gloriosa dei Frari. In the latter, his tombstone in the St. Ambrose Chapel, the third to the left of the choir, is a less impressive monument than a eulogy by Matteo Camberlotti in 1644 which pays tribute to the way Monteverdi's genius radiates in all directions. In the Frari church, typically enough, the tombs of Titian and Canova are readily pointed out by most guides, whereas that of Monteverdi (recently restored, with the birth date erroneously chiseled as 1565 instead of 1567) will be found only by the visitor's initiative.

The Teatro San Cassiano no longer stands, although the location is easily identified by the parish across the Canale Grande and a bit south from the Ca' d'Oro. But two seventeenth-century opera houses are still accessible to the twentieth-century traveler, although he is not likely to hear any operas in either of them. The older of the two opened in 1661 under the patronage of the illustrious Vendramin family. A contemporary French journal, the *Mercure Galant,* describes it as "fort grand, fort beau, tout paint et doré de neuf, et des plus considérables de Venise. Il contient cinq rangs de palcs, trente-trois à chaque rang." ("Very big, very beautiful, all painted and gilded anew, and among the most important in Venice. It contains five tiers of boxes, thirty-three in each tier.") Originally called Teatro San Salvatore after the parish, it was renamed Teatro Goldoni in 1875, honoring the playwright whose twenty libretti for operas first performed in Venice have been overshadowed by his other accomplishments. Taking the standard walk from San Marco under the arch of the clock tower toward the Rialto, one finds the theater by turning left instead of right before reaching the bridge. The huge house was declared unsafe after the Second World War. A total restoration was begun in 1961; and if the funds do not run out (there were exactly two men on the job in the summer of 1962), the Teatro Goldoni promises to continue its long life with glory and elegance. But even while totally gutted, it is worth a sentimental visit.

The other surviving theater, built in 1678 behind the church of San Giovanni Grisostomo (past the Rialto bridge and the main post office), was the most magnificent of all seventeenth-century Venetian opera houses. Giovanni Bonlini, writing in Venice half a century later about *Le glorie della poesia e della musica,* reports that "it was built within the space of a few months above the ruins of an old building already destroyed by fire with that magnificence appropriate to the house of Grimani. It was once the habitual dwelling of the famous Marco Polo who lived at the end of the thirteenth century, renowned in every age for his far distant travels. Thus, from a pile of memorable ashes one saw, almost unexpectedly in this great capital and true kingdom of marvels, arise this real phoenix of theatres to the glory of poetry and music, which, with the vastness of its superb structure, was able to rival the pomp of ancient Rome and which, with the magnificence of its more than regal dramatic display, has now gained the applause and esteem of the whole world."

The admission of the whole world is still available today

for the price of a movie ticket. The house is well known as the Teatro Malibran; and, since 1919, Hollywood productions have occupied the place once dedicated to premieres by Handel and Gluck and to the voices of Farinelli and La Faustina. Toscanini, also, conducted here at the beginning of his career. From the bridge behind the theater (Ponte del Teatro O Marco Polo) one can read the memorial tablet set on the location of *le case di Marco Polo.* The inside of the theater looks bare (although the whitewash did not reach the ceiling painting), but the preservation of the original architecture should make it easy for the phoenix to rise once more. The report of a Parisian correspondent in Venice, sent home five years after the opening, deserves to be quoted at length if only to give the present-day moviegoer a basis for comparison:

"The theater of St. John Chrysostome is the largest, most beautiful, and richest in the city. The auditorium is surrounded by five tiers of boxes, one on top of the other, thirty-one in each tier. They are embellished by sculptural ornaments in low and high relief, all gilded, representing various kinds of antique vases, shells, animal heads, roses, rosettes, flowers, foliage, and other types of decoration. Below and between each of these boxes are as many human figures depicted in white marble, also in relief and life-sized, holding up the pillars which form the separations between the loges. These are men with clubs, slaves, terms of both sexes, and groups of little children, all placed in such a way that the heaviest and most massive ones are below and the lightest at the top.

"The upper part and the ceiling of the auditorium is painted in the form of a gallery, at one end of which, at the side of the stage, are the arms of the Grimani, and above a glorification of some fabulous divinity, surrounded by a flock of winged children who wind flowers into garlands.

"The stage is thirteen *toises* and three feet [82 ft. 7 in.] in depth by ten *toises* and two feet [63 ft. 6 in.] in width, and of proportional height. Its opening is formed by a great proscenium of the height of the auditorium, in the thickness of which are four boxes on each side of the same symmetry as the others, but much more ornate. In the vault of the proscenium two figures of Fame with their trumpets appear suspended in air, and a Venus in the center caresses a little Cupid.

"An hour before the opening of the theater, the painting of the Venus is withdrawn, leaving a great opening whence descends a kind of chandelier ornamented with four branches of gold and silver work. The chandelier has a height of from twelve to fourteen feet. Its trunk is a great sculptured cartouche of the Grimani coat-of-arms, with a crown of *fleurs-de-lis* and of rays surmounted with pearls. The chandelier carries four great tapers of white wax, which light the auditorium and remain lighted until the curtain is raised. Then the whole machine vanishes, and the proscenium returns to its first stage. As soon as the opera is ended, this machine appears again to light the auditorium and to allow the spectators to leave at their ease and without confusion."

The large number of boxes, five times thirty-three in the Teatro Goldoni, is characteristic of an opera audience that transacted personal and political business during a performance. The French ambassador to Venice assured a friend that all diplomats went to the opera regularly in order to discover secrets that would otherwise remain concealed from them. Hence it is understandable that the doge himself allotted boxes to the heads of foreign missions and personally drew lots to ensure good diplomatic relations by a fair distribution of desirable opera seats.

The complexity of the productions was described by an English tourist, Edward Wright, in the early eighteenth century: "They are very dextrous at the Machinery of their Operas. In one of them Nero presents Tiridates King of Armenia with a Roman show, of which himself makes a part.

The Emperor with the Empress appear in a Triumphal Chariot, drawn by an Elephant. The Head, Trunk, and Eyes of the great Beast move as if alive, and Tiridates believes he is so. When, all of a sudden, as soon as the Emperor and Empress are dismounted and have taken their Seats, the Triumphal Chariot is transform'd into an Amphitheatre, and fill'd with Spectators. The Elephant falls all in pieces, and out of his Belly come a great number of Gladiators, arm'd with Bucklers, which were so many parts of the Elephant's Sides, so that he seems in a moment to be transform'd into a company of arm'd Men, who make a Skirmish, all in time to the Musick."

Not every Venetian approved of elephants in an opera. The nobleman Benedetto Marcello wrote a witty and devastating satire on operatic practices around 1720: *Il Teatro alla Moda* makes good reading to this day. Marcello's "Safe and easy Method of properly composing and producing Italian Operas according to modern practice" is dedicated not only to poets and composers but also to "prompters, copyists, and mothers of lady singers." The first of many "useful and necessary recommendations" to the composer of music is to ignore the rules of good composition. Instead, "the modern composer will show the greatest attentions to all the virtuose of the operas, presenting them all with old cantatas transposed to fit their voices, in addition saying to each one that the opera owes its success to her talent. The same thing he will say to each man in the cast, to each member of the orchestra, to each supernumerary, bear, earthquake, etc."

Benedetto Marcello was a good composer himself. His father and brothers were all very musical. Although he reputedly practiced the violin ten hours a day in his late teens, he obeyed his father's wish to study law in preparation for a respectable diplomatic career. Thus he became a member of the Consiglio dei Quaranta and received various political honors and duties. But he also remained active in literary and musical academies and even gave voice lessons. His compositions were hand-copied across the Alps by his contemporary Johann Sebastian Bach; and his psalm settings, which employed themes borrowed from the Jewish synagogue in Venice, evoked the admiration of Verdi more than a century later. Today the renowned conservatory in the Pisani Palace (near the Campo San Stefano) is named after him. The gondolier who is not likely to have heard any note by Marcello will be quick to inform the tourist floating down the Canale Grande that the house next to the Palazzo Vendramin-Calergi (east of it, to be quite exact, i.e., toward the Rialto) once belonged to the *principe della musica.* There is a little plaque on the wall, but a normal eye can hardly read it from the canal. Although the attention given Benedetto Marcello by his compatriots at the expense of so many other superior composers may be explained by the fact that he came from a patrician family with a house on the Canale Grande, he was doubtless a very well-educated and sensitive humanist. Marcello identified himself on his publications as *nobile Veneto dilettante di contrappunto,* indicating that music was not the main source of his income.

It was so, however, for his contemporary Antonio Vivaldi, who was neither a nobleman nor a dilettante and who did not hesitate to produce in Venice alone twenty-two operas *alla moda.* Nor did he fare badly, for he acted as his own concert manager with a sharp eye on the box office. His father was a violinist at St. Mark's; and he must have transmitted his excellence to his son, for both are singled out by the *Visitor's Guide* to Venice in 1713 as being "among the best who play the violin." Antonio Vivaldi was known as the *prete rosso* (red priest); but in 1737, when he was about sixty years old, the ecclesiastical authorities of Ferrara forbade him to visit their city and produce an opera because he was a priest "who did not say Mass"; and his red hair was associated with his hot temperament and prolific creativity, of which three red-headed brothers in jail and about fifty operas and five hundred concertos in score are only a partial representation. The quality of his music may be judged by the fact that Johann Sebastian Bach transcribed at least ten Vivaldi works for his own instruction and his listeners' pleasure.

The locale of Venice is so prominent in Vivaldi's life that it can easily stimulate the traveler's imagination today. Walking away from San Marco on the Riva degli Schiavoni, one soon reaches the church of the Pietà. The building was reconstructed after Vivaldi's death; but on the site, and adjoining it, stood the Ospedale della Pietà, an orphan asylum for girls where Vivaldi was employed as a music master for most of his life. Anyone doubting the musical satisfaction derived from this kind of position will be set right by letters from the French magistrate and scholar Charles de Brosses, whose visit to Venice in 1739 coincided with Vivaldi's activity: "The Ospedali have the best music here. There are four of them, all for illegitimate or orphaned girls whose parents cannot support them. These are brought up at the State's expense and trained exclusively in music. Indeed they sing like angels, play the violin, flute, organ, oboe, cello, bassoon—in short no instrument is large enough to frighten them. They are cloistered like nuns. The performances are entirely their own and each concert is composed of about forty girls. I swear nothing is more charming than to see a young pretty nun, dressed in white, a sprig of pomegranate blossom behind one ear, leading the orchestra and beating time with all the grace and precision imaginable . . . Where I go most often and enjoy myself most is the Ospedale della Pietà. It ranks first for the perfection of its symphonies. What well-drilled execution! That is the only place to hear a first attack from the strings such as, quite undeservedly, the Paris opera is renowned for."

The traveler can see for himself; for Gabriele Bella's

painting, "Cantata Delle Putte Delli Ospitalli," in the Querini-Stampalia Gallery is an accurate reproduction of the eighteenth-century Venetian scene. Vivaldi's autonomy in musical matters and his freedom to experiment were curtailed, at worst, by the presence of chaperones at his lessons to make sure that the girls "behave with the necessary discipline," and by his having to cast a girl for the role of Holofernes, among others, in his treatment of the Judith story.

What musical scenes could a modern De Brosses report? The band concerts on the Piazza San Marco are amusing; the flurry of special musical performances during the tourist season and the September Biennale is commercial; the opera season, short; and good church music, practically nonexistent. The visitor's imagination will have to fill in many details to reconcile the present lull with the past glory of musical Venice, the stripped movie house Malibran with the Baroque opera house San Giovanni Grisostomo. The same imagination, however, will be staggered by the intact perfection and beauty of the current opera house, the Teatro La Fenice. A visit is obligatory, not merely because La Fenice is one of the most ingratiating attractions of Venice, but because it makes an easy claim to being the most elegant and satisfactory opera house anywhere. Ticket holders may alight from gondolas at a special portal for a performance or may also reach it on foot by leaving the piazza at the far end from the cathedral and turning right after passing San Moisè and the back of the Bauer Grünwald Hotel. If there is a performance, even in an unintelligible language, nothing should keep one from attending and surrounding one's self with the visual and acoustical pleasures, the physical and spiritual comforts, of the house. If there is no performance, a sympathetic attendant at the stage door (on the side to the right of the front) is likely to yield to a few hundred lire and an expression of genuine interest.

The Teatro La Fenice opened in 1792 with *I Giuochi d'Agrigento* by Giovanni Paisiello, probably the most popular opera composer of the day. Rossini, Donizetti, and Bellini all were helped along on their respective careers in the early nineteenth century by premieres and performances at La Fenice. When Donizetti, quite famous by 1843, asked for 30,000 francs (a huge sum) to write a new opera for the 1844 carnival season in Venice, the management of La Fenice commissioned the thirty-year-old Verdi as a substitute. *Ernani* was a gigantic success, and Verdi's name remained associated with the Teatro La Fenice for the remainder of the century. The premiere of *Rigoletto* followed in 1851, that of *La Traviata* in 1853. From his Albergo d'Europa, now the Hotel Europa e Britannia, on the Canale Grande, Verdi wrote to his friend Emanuele Muzio: "*La Traviata* last night was a fiasco. Is the fault mine or the singers'? Time will judge." It had judged before Verdi wrote another opera for La Fenice, *Simon Boccanegra* in 1857. Verdi was still alive when Toscanini, a youngster in his twenties, introduced *Falstaff* and *La Forza del Destino* to the Teatro La Fenice and to Venice.

In the same building, on Christmas Eve 1882, Richard Wagner celebrated Cosima's birthday by performing his C-major symphony, which he had written exactly fifty years earlier. Only a few friends were present, among them Liszt and Humperdinck. It was Wagner's last appearance as a conductor. He had spent the winter in a lavish rented suite in the Palazzo Vendramin-Calergi, the massive structure of 1509 on the Canale Grande between the Ca' d'Oro and what is today the railroad station. There he died on 13 February 1883.

VERONA

THERE ARE CITIES that act on musicians like sirup on flies and stimulate musical activities like wine. Vienna and Paris are good examples. There are other cities, however, just as old, beautiful, and rich in culture, that seem to have kept out all musical experiences like a deaf person. Verona is a case in point. Neither Dante nor San Zeno managed to break the spell. Verona is mentioned here only as a piquant example of a sophisticated but totally unmusical town. There is nothing musical to report.

The foundation of an ambitious Accademia Filarmonica in 1543 only emphasizes the point: all well-meant, high-pressured, and richly endowed efforts produced barely a musical mouse. The best outside composers and instrumentalists, engaged to cultivate music among the twenty-nine selected members, left no imprint on Verona except by the deposit of an instrument collection.

The two organs facing each other across the nave of the Duomo testify to the influence of Venice no less than the column of St. Mark on the Piazza delle Erbe.

VICENZA

THE TEATRO OLIMPICO, Palladio's last work, was opened on 3 March 1585 with a performance of *King Oedipus* by Sophocles. The building, the architect, and the play have remained familiar and illustrious through the centuries. The music played for the occasion, although of the first order and of special historic interest, is seldom mentioned.

In line with the importance of the event, the best available artists were hired by the Accademia Olimpica, the literary society which had planned the erection of the theater and which was sponsoring the opening night. (Almost exactly two hundred years later, Goethe attended a meeting of the same academy and recorded his pleasure at the intelligence and liveliness of the discussion.) Vicenza belonged to the Venetian republic at the time. To secure appropriate music for the new translation of "the world's most excellent tragedy" (as a Renaissance letter describing the opening night calls it), it seemed obvious to commission the most famous and respected composer in Venice, the first organist at the San Marco Cathedral, Andrea Gabrieli, then about seventy years old.

Andrea Gabrieli had been born in the Venetian republic and had sung as a boy in the choir of San Marco under the great Adrian Willaert. For a short while, he was organist at San Geremia in Venice (the church with cupola and campanile on the Canale Grande halfway between the railroad station and the Palazzo Vendramin-Calergi). We know that Andrea Gabrieli traveled widely. Thus he was a member of the musical ensemble which went under the direction of Orlando Lasso to the coronation of Maximilian II in Frankfurt in 1562. His commission for Vicenza was only one in a row of similar public tasks that attest to his high reputation. It was he, for instance, whom the Venetian government asked to celebrate in music the famous victory over the Turks at Lepanto in 1571 (where Cervantes, fighting as a private, lost forever the use of his left hand, "for the greater glory of the right," in his own phrase; and which every visitor to the Doge's Palace in Venice remembers as the topic of the largest painting of them all). Although Gabrieli employed in his compositions all musical forms of the day, he was, and still is, particularly famous for his handling of double choirs—two separate choirs (sometimes even more) singing in the same composition against each other, with each other, now contrasting in range or timbre or dynamics, now combining for mass effects. The architecture of San Marco in Venice with its two organs particularly favored this kind of technique (which can be found again in Bach's *Passion According to St. Matthew*).

For the opening night in Vicenza it was Gabrieli's task to compose the music for the choruses. The Olympic Academy, typical of the Renaissance revival of classic art, was correct in assuming that the Greek dramas were originally sung, at least in part, and that they were in effect operas rather than plays. Gabrieli's mastery in writing for double choirs was perfectly suited to the structure of a Greek drama, in which the chorus enters, recites, and acts in two distinct sections. Usually there is a strophe sung by one half of the chorus, answered in a parallel antistrophe by the other half, and finally crowned by an epode rendered by the whole chorus. Andrea Gabrieli proved his understanding of the problem of assisting the Sophocles drama when he let the rhythm of the words govern that of the music. In order not to obscure the text, he abandoned the traditional independence of the various voices in favor of so-called "homophonic" scanning. This technique, in which all members of a chorus pronounce every syllable or word at the same time, was more "modern" in Gabrieli's time than one might imagine today. It ensured total intelligibility of the text in large halls.

A long letter exists by a man, Filippo Pigafetta, who attended the opening night at the Teatro Olimpico and described the evening in detail to a distant aristocratic friend. A few excerpts may be quoted:

"If my hand would be obedient to my mind, as Michel Agnolo Buonarroti, the eminent painter, sculptor, and architect used to say, and if the social activities, the flow of wine, and the bustle of the carnival permit me, I would like to please Your Highness and Your friends by describing the theatrical pomp and the magnificence of the tragedy which yesterday was recited in this city. . . . Palladio, wanting to leave behind him a perfect work of art, convinced the Academicians of Vicenza, called the Olimpici, that, in view of the fact that their noble institution many times recited eclogues, pastorals, comedies, tragedies, and other such pleasures for the enjoyment of the people, they should build a theater according to the ancient custom of the Greeks and Romans. . . . Little by little they have brought to an end the masterly and admirable work of art. The theater can easily accommodate 3,000 spectators. It is such a charming sight that everybody is usually pleased by it because of the exquisite beauty of its proportions. . . . Just think, Your most illustrious Lordship, a complete building designed by Palladio in the last years of his life and in the full mastery of his knowledge. . . . In this theater, which cost 18,000 ducats with all its appurtenances, the Academicians produced—in tune with the edifice—the noblest tragedy ever written, *Oedipus the King* . . . by the Athenian poet Sophocles, exalted above all others by Aristotle. Thus in the most famous theater of the world, the world's most excellent tragedy was given. . . . The choral music was composed by Andrea Gabrieli, organist of St. Mark's. . . . There were eighty stage costumes. The tragedy has nine speaking parts, and the cast had been doubled by understudies to provide for an emergency. Two of the players, the King and the Queen, were magnificently dressed in gold cloth. Accommodations had been courteously provided for about 2,000 gentlemen from Venice and the State as well as from other countries, not counting the others, so that on the streets of Vicenza one could see nothing but noblemen and noblewomen, carriages, horses, and strangers who had come to attend the performance . . . There was an incredible display of kindness on the part of the Academicians toward all the guests, when the latter reached the entrance, where quite a crowd had assembled, and when they were shown their seats inside, receiving, upon request, refreshing wines and fruits . . . There were more than 3,000 spectators. People came early . . . The performance began at 7:30 and was over by 11. Some, for instance, I and some of my friends, stayed there perhaps eleven hours, not getting tired at all. . . . When the time had come to lower the curtain, a very sweet smell of perfume made itself felt to indicate that in the city of Thebes, according to the ancient legend, incense was burned to placate the wrath of the gods. Then there was a sound of trumpets and drums, and four squibs exploded. In a twinkle of an eye the curtain fell before the stage. I can hardly express in words, nor can it be imagined, how great the joy was, and the infinite pleasure felt by the spectators when they, after a moment of stunned surprise, watched the prologue, and when the sound of harmonized voices and divers instruments could be heard from a distance behind the scenic façade . . . The actors are of the best sort . . . The King had a guard of twenty-four archers dressed in Turkish fashion . . . The chorus consisted of 15 persons, seven on each side, and their leader in the center. The chorus spoke, as is required, in pleasing unison, so that almost all the words could be clearly understood, an effect which is very difficult to achieve in tragedies. . . ."

SELECTED BIBLIOGRAPHY

THE TRAVELER IN Italy whose musical appetite has been whetted will find good additional information in the books listed below. The bibliography has been restricted to books in English readily available in the United States. The author gratefully acknowleges his indebtedness to source material contained in some of these books.

The compositions of older composers, whenever not commercially distributed, are represented in complete editions in most college and university libraries, as well as in many public and private libraries. Current phonograph catalogues are likely to contain the names of most composers mentioned in this book.

Biographies, Letters, Memoirs

Memoirs of Hector Berlioz, ed. Ernest Newman. New York: Alfred A. Knopf, Inc., 1932.

Berlioz and the Romantic Century, Jacques Barzun. 2 vols. Boston: Little, Brown & Co., 1950.

Bizet, Winton Dean. ("The Master Musicians.") London: J. M. Dent and Sons, 1948.

Brahms, Peter Latham. ("The Master Musicians.") New York: Pellegrini and Cudahy, 1949.

Charles Burney: Musical Tours in Europe, ed. Percy A. Scholes. 2 vols. London: Oxford University Press, Inc., 1959.

Corelli. His Life, His Work, Marc Pincherle, translated from the French by E. M. Russell. New York: W. W. Norton & Company, Inc., 1956.

Monsieur Croche the Dilettante Hater, Claude Debussy, translated from the French by B. N. Langdon Davies. New York: Dover Publications, Inc., 1962.

Debussy, His Life and Mind, Edward Lockspeiser, Vol. I. New York: Cassell & Company Ltd., 1962.

Gluck, Alfred Einstein, translated from the German by Eric Blom. ("The Master Musicians.") London: J. M. Dent and Sons, 1954.

Liszt, Sacheverell Sitwell. New York: Philosophical Library, Inc., 1956.

Felix Mendelssohn: Letters, ed. G. Selden-Goth. New York: Pantheon Books, Inc., 1945.

Claudio Monteverdi, Life and Works, Hans F. Redlich, translated from the German by Kathleen Dale. London and New York: Oxford University Press, 1952.

Monteverdi. Creator of Modern Music, Leo Schrade. New York: W. W. Norton & Company, Inc., 1950.

The Letters of Mozart and His Family, ed. and translated by Emily Anderson. 3 vols. New York: The Macmillan Company, 1938.

Mozart, Eric Blom. ("The Master Musicians.") London: J. M. Dent and Sons, 1935.

Palestrina, Henry Coates. ("The Master Musicians.") London: J. M. Dent and Sons, 1938.

Puccini. A Critical Biography, Mosco Carner. New York: Alfred A. Knopf, Inc., 1959.

Rossini: A Study in Tragi-comedy, Francis Toye. New York: Alfred A. Knopf, Inc., 1947.

Domenico Scarlatti (rev. ed.), Ralph Kirkpatrick. Princeton: Princeton University Press, 1955.

Verdi: The Man in His Letters, ed. Franz Werfel and Paul Stefan, translated from the German by Edward Downes. New York: L. B. Fischer Publishing Corp., 1942.

Giuseppe Verdi: His Life and Works, Francis Toye. New York: Alfred A. Knopf, Inc., 1946.

Vivaldi, Genius of the Baroque, Marc Pincherle, translated from the French by Christopher Hatch. New York: W. W. Norton & Company, Inc., 1957.

The Life of Richard Wagner, Ernest Newman. 4 vols. New York: Alfred A. Knopf, Inc., 1933–46.

General

Music in the Baroque Era, Manfred F. Bukofzer. New York: W. W. Norton & Company, Inc., 1947.

The Italian Madrigal, Alfred Einstein. 3 vols. Princeton: Princeton University Press, 1949.

A Short History of Opera, Donald J. Grout. New York: Columbia University Press, 1947.

A History of Western Music, Donald J. Grout. New York: W. W. Norton & Company, Inc., 1960.

Great Opera Houses, Spike Hughes. London: Weidenfeld and Nicolson, 1956.

Italian Violin Makers, Karel Jalovec. New York: Crown Publishers, Inc., 1957.

A Source Book in Theatrical History, Alois M. Nagler. New York: Dover Publications, 1959.

Music in the Middle Ages, Gustave Reese. New York: W. W. Norton & Company, Inc., 1940.

Music in the Renaissance, Gustave Reese. New York: W. W. Norton & Company, Inc., 1954.
Source Readings in Music History, ed. Oliver Strunk. New York: W. W. Norton & Company, Inc., 1950.
Venetian Opera in the Seventeenth Century, Simon T. Worsthorne. Oxford: Clarendon Press, 1954.
Music at Court, Alan Yorke-Long. London: Weidenfeld and Nicolson, 1954.

INDEX